Britons Abroad

Britons Abroad (1968) takes the lid off nine 1960s package tours, mainly in Europe, revealing the kind of people taking part, what they got for their money and the adventures that befell them. Air tours, ski parties, coach tours, villa holidays, student tours and ocean cruises are among the holidays that come under scrutiny.

Britons Abroad

A Report on the Package Tour

Charles Owen

Routledge
Taylor & Francis Group

First published in 1968
by Routledge & Kegan Paul Limited

This edition first published in 2025 by Routledge
4 Park Square, Milton Park, Abingdon, Oxon, OX14 4RN

and by Routledge
605 Third Avenue, New York, NY 10017

Routledge is an imprint of the Taylor & Francis Group, an informa business

© 1968 Charles Owen

Publisher's Note
The publisher has gone to great lengths to ensure the quality of this reprint but points out that some imperfections in the original copies may be apparent.

Disclaimer
The publisher has made every effort to trace copyright holders and welcomes correspondence from those they have been unable to contact.

A Library of Congress record exists under LCCN: 68097215

ISBN: 978-1-032-95586-5 (hbk)
ISBN: 978-1-003-58561-9 (ebk)
ISBN: 978-1-032-95587-2 (pbk)

Book DOI 10.4324/9781003585619

Britons Abroad

A Report on the
Package Tour

by CHARLES OWEN

ROUTLEDGE & KEGAN PAUL

First published 1968
by Routledge & Kegan Paul Limited
Broadway House, 68–74, Carter Lane
London, E.C.4

Printed in Great Britain
by C. Tinling & Co. Ltd
Liverpool, London and Prescot

SBN 7100 4337 6

For Caroline and Rupert

Contents

vii

STOP PRESS   DEVALUATION

Since this book went to press, the pound sterling has been devalued. The effect of this would be to increase by about ten per cent the prices of the tours given in chapters one, three, four, six and seven. Those in chapters two, five and eight would remain unchanged.

JANUARY 1968

Preface
Author's Note

This book takes a quizzical look at nine package tours abroad for British holiday makers. All but one are to destinations in Europe. Their character and cost vary widely; their appeal, between them, is to almost every taste and every age.

All the tours took place in 1966 and 1967, being chosen and described specially for this book. I joined five of them as an ordinary member of the party, paying the full price, taking care not to disclose the object of my presence; my representatives on the other trips were equally inconspicuous, and I have edited their reports without bias.

While the main purpose of the book is entertainment,

the accounts include comment on values and facilities. Some of the tour promoters, and their arrangements, are praised and others criticised. The behaviour and adventures of fellow-tourists are fully described. To avoid hurt feelings, however, the identities of firms, vehicles and lodgings have, for the most part, been disguised, and the names or backgrounds of the more prominent individuals altered. In chapter eight, in particular, as cruise connoisseurs may well see through the *Old Lady's* camouflage, care has been taken to change some of the characters, notably those of the lovers, and to distort some of the minor details. All the stories are otherwise true.

I should like to thank my wife, Felicity, for bringing back the report given in chapter four. I was represented on the student trip recorded in chapter three by Patricia Franklin, an English girl, accompanied by her American friend, Joan Harris, and on the other tour mentioned in this chapter, by Shirley Fry. I am obliged to all three for their help. I am grateful to my young daughter, Caroline, for chaperoning me on the voyage logged in chapter eight and to my son, Rupert, for keeping me company on the jaunt described in chapter seven. I acknowledge advice or assistance received from Jill Gough, Elizabeth Jupp, Anne Porter and Marie-Christine von Reibnitz. I am indebted to Cherry Burrows who, besides working her passage on two of the tours, contributed the saga forming chapter six, and did nearly all the typing.

CHARLES OWEN

Foreword
The Qualm Before
the Storm

WE may be individualists at home but most of us, when we venture abroad, seem loath to go it alone. We prefer to be organised. Fortunately, we are not starved of opportunity. At the start of each year, newspapers and magazines burst forth in a flowering of holiday advertisements inviting us to a multitude of destinations, by diverse means, at bargain prices. When we answer an advertisement we receive a detailed catalogue, replete with enticing coloured photographs of sunny beaches, lakes, mountains, hotels, aeroplanes, ships, girls and laughing, carefree customers.

We choose a tour and pay the deposit; nearer the time, we settle the rest of the bill and receive our marching orders. We are now in the care of the tour operator or his agent. Our money in his pocket, we have only to turn up at the given departure point; all the rest —transport, accommodation, side-trips and entertainment—should be doled out to us, precisely, as forecast in his programme. We are the package or the party or the all-in tourist and, today, we form the bulk of the foreign-bound travelling public.

By choice, I belong with the minority. I prefer to plan my own journeys. This is not invariably more expensive. It is often possible to make part-use of tour facilities; one may save also by sleeping cheap and buying meals or picnics as and when they are needed, instead of paying full *en pension* terms, and by night travel between one location and the next; and one can, after all, stay a shorter time at a disappointing destination. But one must be ready sometimes to pay a little more for freedom and spontaneity.

A year or two ago I wrote a book for my present publisher about some of my independent travels. The journeys themselves were, of course, the main part of the fun. The book sold quite well and, when my publisher hinted benignly that a sequel might be welcome, I was pleasantly surprised. But I reckoned without the quaint sense of humour of publishers.

Over salmon mayonnaise at the Garrick Club, a sardonic smile half-prepared me for the bombshell. 'Could you bear to take a look at the other side of the coin?' asked my publisher. 'We think that a book about package travel might make a good sequel—there should be a fairly large public for this kind of thing. But, clearly, you must first go on some of the tours yourself. We feel sure you could turn them to good account.'

Strawberries and cream proved a spur to my host's inspiration. I was to select an assortment of package tours among the many offered to Britons by British promoters. They were all to be overseas tours—of varying character, involving different forms of travel and different destinations. My publisher was gently but firmly persuasive and, subdued by a glass of port, I came finally under his spell.

As we were leaving the club, he had an afterthought. 'You know, it may not be quite the ordeal you expect. Some of your fears or, one might say, prejudices may prove to be unfounded. But many people undoubtedly share them and it would be interesting if you were to set them down in a foreword *before* you started the first trip.' As his taxi drew up at the door, my publisher added: 'And, at the end of the book, when the journeys have been done, you might add a piece confessing how right or wrong you were in your anticipation. It could be quite revealing.' He waved good-bye and was gone.

Out of such labour this book was born. In the ensuing weeks I collected the catalogues of more than thirty British travel agents and tour operators. The all-in holidays covered by this library of enthusiastic literature ranges world-wide and, in price, from £550 16s for a month's tour of China to £12 12s for a two-day trip to Holland. I delved deeply and wearily into my collection, small print and all, and so far, after a lengthy process of elimination, I have selected six tours.

As I write, the first of these is due to start within a month. I view it with some apprehension. It is a motor coach 'cruise' and it will last nine days. It begins at Boulogne, after the sea crossing from Dover, and it takes in Brussels, the Rhineland, two Swiss resorts, and

3

Paris. We are to have two consecutive nights at Interlaken; otherwise we spend only a single night at each main stop.

It may be a very jolly party. I imagine we shall be rather an aged lot, the men sweating it out in fawn linen jackets and the women in dainty flower-patterned frocks. As our baggage is strictly limited and there is little time for clothes-washing *en route*, one hopes for a well-ventilated coach. I dread the daily claustrophobia; most of all, I dread the facetious monotone of our courier's commentary as we speed down the *autobahns* or twist our way among the mountains.

I am sure my fellow-passengers will be stoic and tolerant folk whose main technique with foreigners will be to thank them endlessly for small services. I have no doubt that smiling gratitude will be expressed to each taciturn receptionist for the pleasure of queuing, on registering and when the bedrooms are allocated.

The tour operator expects us to occupy double rooms, sharing with a member of the same sex. My companion will wear flannel pyjamas; if he has any, he will surely grind his teeth while he sleeps. Or, given only one tooth mug to each bedroom, there will be a problem over dentures. I abhor queues; it is bad enough to wait in line at a reception desk but it is even worse to take one's anxious turn in the morning for the lavatory. The coach may leave before we have all had time to do our duty. And what happens if one of us is taken short *en route*?

I was discussing this peril the other day with a woman friend, an inveterate tourist, who suffered her *moment de crise* when the motor coach in which she was travelling was at the highest point of an Alpine pass. In harassed tones she begged the driver to stop. She alighted, walked back a furlong and, hidden from view by a boulder, achieved the relief for which she had been longing. She hastened to retrace her steps—but the coach had not waited. On such trips, evidently, the schedule is paramount. The lady managed to hitch a lift from a passing car and caught up with the coach in the next town, where it had stopped for lunch. I hope that any similar predicament on my trip will end as happily.

Undoubtedly the night in Paris is to be the highlight. I can hardly wait for this, and not only because it is the last night of the trip. I believe we are to be conveyed around a few of the gaudier cabarets, a provocation to British *sang-froid*—and a prelude, I fear, to some pretty gruesome reminiscences by my room-mate as we lie sleepless in the breaking dawn.

I am sure the chief consolation will be the affable good nature of my travel companions. We shall be cooped up together, more or less, for nine days and I expect to make new friends. It is a wonderful chance to know, vicariously, a host of children, grandchildren, aunts, uncles and witty neighbours. I have asked for a seat neither within repartee distance of the courier nor over the back wheels. I wonder if such a seat exists, and who will occupy the other half of it? An experience like this could change one's whole life.

A fortnight or so after the coach cruise I am due to set out on a two-centre package 'holiday' visiting Palma and Sitges. Few resorts are better known to Britons or more frequented by them. Palma is often the first stop overseas for the newly-itinerant northerner and has a unique appeal for almost every class and pocket, from honeymooners to pensioners.

Travel is to be by air and accommodation, including victuals, will be in hotels somewhat below the top category. The Spaniards have a gift for large scale tourism but it must be difficult to make the endlessly repeated smiles of welcome seem genuine. Each resort adjoins areas of great beauty and ample amenity and the best thing about this tour may be the ability to escape from it between meals and wander at will.

Full pension is a serious handicap, not only because of the tie but because the pre-paid food and service will, to say the least, lack distinction. The modern tourist hotel in Spain is shorn of frills, designed on the assumption that the guests will be most of the time in bed or out of doors. The dining room, if we have to eat indoors, with its tiled floor and bare wooden furniture, will echo with banal chatter and the clink of cutlery; the unhurried waiters will be familiar, with a hint of condescension, escaping frequently into the kitchen to hide their boredom.

I expect the company to be unexciting and, when caught off guard, lugubrious in manner. It needs an effort to maintain a genuine conviviality throughout fourteen days of aimless activity. When I think of Sitges, where I once spent an evening, I recall the sunset migration, from the beaches to the bodegas, of droves of middle-aged Englishmen in their white open-necked shirts, rolled up to the elbows, khaki shorts and army-type gym shoes. To drink sherry among one's compatriots in haunts unfrequented by the natives seems a tame way to live it up, but there must be some magic in this and the kindred pursuits enjoyed by the package tourist which has so far escaped me. I shall approach the experience with a clear head—and an open mind.

6

While I am busy on these two opening jaunts, some-one is representing me on a students' package tour to Turkey and Greece. I tried out all my disguises but could find none which would survive the scrutiny of the National Union of Students under whose auspices this trip is taking place. My deputy is a rather gorgeous girl from RADA; it seems a shame that we cannot go together.

In some respects I envy her not at all. Accompanied by an actress friend, she begins with three continuous days in a train, second class, and the accommodation at the destinations will be fairly rudimentary. But the excursion offers a fine opportunity, on a modest budget, to visit these two countries and to live for a while in fairly close contact with their citizens. The days (and the nights) are long and the Greeks, at least, understand that life is here to be lived, in full, during every waking minute. Alas, this is probably the most attractive trip in my book—and I cannot make it!

At the same season, someone else will kindly deputise for me on a visit to Italy, this being a 'circular' tour embracing Venice, Florence and Rome. My wife, on this occasion, is the lucky victim; I am unable to be in two places at once and time presses. The Italians are the traditional masters of package tourism and, as they are also a never-failing success with ladies of every hue and contour, I have few qualms about the fate and, perhaps, the adventures awaiting my spouse as she goes about my business. Her economical frame of mind is an asset for, where I tend to avoid descending below the second category of hotel, she can find solace in a *pensione*. Her journey has a fairly substantial culture content and this, apart from the venue, will help to distinguish it from the

B

others. The travel is to be partly by air, partly by train and partly by motor coach, and is to last about ten days.

A welcome break follows these early explorations, while I attend to other matters and start turning my notes, and my roving correspondents' reports, into chapters of this book. Then, it will be Christmas and, soon after this festival, I plan to sample an all-in ski tour with Kitzbuehel, in Austria, as the main locale. This promises to be a gay enough trip if one can stand the snow; I suffer the slight handicap of being a non-skier. We are to travel in a special train from one of the Channel ports overnight to the destination. I understand that this conveyance offers couchettes, a food car and a carriage equipped as a night club. I have never danced in a speeding train but it might be worth a try; the twist and the shake, at least, should not seem out of place.

I expect Kitzbuehel to be stimulating for, as in most ski-ing resorts, a great throng of extroverted people will be thrown together with gregarious intent. While most of them are risking their limbs upon the slopes the dowagers and I will browse among the tea-rooms and the souvenir shops, saving our energies for *le après-ski*. By common consent this is when the real fun begins, and I hope that my well-nursed energies will enable me to compete with the pink-cheeked hordes in their nocturnal frolics.

Austria will be the fifth trip in the series and I am sure that what I shall really deserve after all that, is a holiday . . . but one must struggle on, somehow, in the interests of literature. Publishers are hard task-masters and must be humoured.

My sixth trip, at least, should make mine envious and maybe the telling of it will give a little vicarious pleasure to my readers. This is to be an ocean cruise in one of the

8

world's biggest liners. It is to last eight days, and its sole port of call will be Las Palmas in the Canary Islands. For those who wish for undiluted pleasure in relaxed surroundings, their initiative yielded to capable organisers, the cares of the world forgotten, there is nothing to beat the life at sea.

I have travelled fairly often by ocean liners on their scheduled voyages but this will be my first fling in a cruising version. No doubt the amenities will be much the same but I expect the officers and the crew to be at their jauntiest. If we are not jollied along throughout our waking hours, these stalwarts will feel that they have failed us. The occasion provides the opportunity for even the most staid among us to engage in youthful frolic without feeling bashful or conspicuous. There will be organised sports and games, raffles, lotteries, bingo, films and matey, elbow-jogging dancing, Paul Jones and all. Between whiles there will be the sun decks, the swim pools, the bars, the barrow loads of food—and occasional moments of repose in one's cabin, wondering what larks are being missed.

The first evening is the difficult one, for shyness and incapacity are not immediately overcome. It is an anxious moment for the socially ambitious, too soon to judge who belongs to whom. Predatory bachelors and spinster birds of prey eye one another warily. A lucky seat at the right dining table can make a world of difference.

I recall one transatlantic trip where the passengers were predominantly elderly. The band, on sailing night, did its best and all the officers seemed to be on duty, trying to drag unwilling women to the dance floor. It was a bit of a flop and I was quite glad to go early to bed.

Six nights later, our destination just beyond the horizon, the scene was transformed. It was gala night; the sea and its mystique had done its work. One could hardly get on to the dance floor. Even the nonagenarians had found a niche upon it, and one officer had difficulty in restraining a gallant old lady in her wheel chair from joining the throng. Yes, I am looking forward to my sea cruise.

I have not yet chosen the seventh and eighth ingredients of this book. If the money holds out, these will complete my stint. I prefer to wait and see how the first six go and, also, what our government does about the travel allowance.

My eye is tentatively on various possibilities, some in the Sterling area and others not. There is always Malta though, if I have had a surfeit of good things in distant places, I may settle for a short, sharp tour of the Dutch bulb fields. Or for a quiet wine-tasting house party in France, perhaps. On the other hand, I do feel somewhat tempted by the hopes of romance held out by those who organise bachelor holidays. Some of the more glamorous and better-equipped holiday camps on Mediterranean shores have a certain appeal. Alternatively, I might opt for a combined air and coach tour of Eire, or a sea and rail tour of Scandinavia.

For the purpose of this foreword it matters little. Enough prejudices and apprehensions have been aired— and, by the time I embark upon numbers seven and eight, I may well have become an ardent package tour addict.

Chapter One
Ordeal by Coach

OUR guide assembled us in the customs hall at Boulogne, within striking distance of the public lavatories. After a brief greeting, he urged immediate use of the facilities. There was a moment's hesitation; then, slowly, sheepishly, the ladies filed through the door on the left, while the gentlemen took their turn to the right.

There were forty of us, a subdued and reticent group, uncertain of our fate. Our faces brightened as we emerged from the lavatories, as though we had passed our first test. A little Canadian at my elbow said he felt the trip promised well for we were obviously in firm hands and, when venturing into Europe, it was surely sensible to yield the initiative to an experienced native.

This remark symbolised the act of surrender we were about to make to the whims and commands of our guide and mentor. I will call him Michel. He is a spruce Belgian of uncertain age, a genial manner masking a will of iron. Michel soon formed us into a crocodile and, satisfied that we were correctly bunched in double ranks, he led us from the customs hall, along the quayside to the waiting coach. There, in the reverse sequence of our seat numbers, we were admitted two-by-two into our four-wheeled ark.

Meanwhile, our baggage had found its way to the coach and was being loaded deftly by our French driver, Jean. An affable, always-smiling man of few words, Jean was of more interest to us at this early stage than Michel, since our driver, presumably, would exercise the greater power of life and death in the coming days.

But we were soon to learn that the mantle of true responsibility was Michel's. He was the captain and Jean merely the helmsman. When we were clear of Boulogne, Michel took up his microphone to issue our sailing orders for the next tack of the voyage. We were obliged to sit up, primly, and take notice. As one of the passengers rose to fold his wife's coat and lodge it in the rack Michel interrupted his commentary. The silence was pointed. It was broken by some muttered conversation at the rear of the coach. Michel barked sternly into the microphone. 'When I have announcements to make,' he insisted, 'you will all kindly give me your attention—it is important for everyone to hear me.'

We were now cowed, chastened, and, I dare say, feeling a bit homesick. It was like the first day of a new term at school and Michel, evidently, meant it that way. He proclaimed that we would shortly halt for a tea-break. He told us how much our tea would cost, and in which currencies we could pay for it. He described the layout of the restaurant, the location of the lavatories, how the doors were marked, and what to tip the attendant. He advised strongly that the amenities be used, his tone of voice making disobedience seem unwise.

So, upon arrival and again, for luck, before departure, the entire party did its duty. This was to be the pattern at every stop throughout the coming days. With practice and discipline, we were gradually to improve our productivity; whereas, at Boulogne, our first shambling effort occupied well over twenty minutes, nine days later all forty of us, a highly-skilled team, could manage our joint and several exercises of nature in fourteen minutes flat.

Worse shocks were to come. We understood, from our printed itinerary, that we were due to leave Brussels at 08.00 hours next day but, as though meting out punishment to recalcitrant pupils, Michel, in one of his microphonic outbursts that first afternoon, announced a programme for the night and morning which included penal variants of his own invention. The intended routine was given out as an instruction; there was no scope for argument or objection.

'On arrival at our hotel in Brussels,' snapped Michel, 'you will kindly assemble in the foyer where I will issue individual cards. Your room numbers will be shown on the cards. Your main baggage, when unloaded, will be placed outside the doors of your respective bedrooms. You will leave your coats and hand-baggage in the care of the *concierge*. You must then proceed to the dining-room where your dinner will be served promptly at 18.30

hours. You will not have time to go to your bedrooms before dinner.'

We cringed inwardly, awaiting the next swish of Michel's cane. 'After dinner you may proceed to your rooms. You will be free for the evening, but I will later recommend certain short excursions which you might wish to make. These, of course, will be charged extra. I advise you to go early to bed. We are to resume our journey tomorrow at 07.30 hours for I have decided to spend extra time at Cologne, where we will stop for the afternoon break, so that you may have ample opportunity both to see the cathedral and to change your currencies.'

A docile gloom now pervaded the coach as Michel continued, 'You will each receive a call by telephone at 06.00 hours, and your main baggage must be placed, ready, outside the doors of your bedrooms by 06.40 hours. Breakfast will be served in the dining-room at 06.45 hours precisely. You should bring your coats and hand-baggage to the dining-room, as it will not be permitted for you to return to your bedrooms after breakfast. Everyone should be in his seat aboard the coach by 07.25 hours.'

We turned inland from Ostend and headed up the motorway for Brussels. There was some petulant muttering but no real sign of revolt. The new term had started and mum was beyond call. At least, we could look forward, nine days hence, to the holidays.

As the tour progressed, Michel gradually relaxed his grip upon us and, from being the stern schoolmaster, he became our ever-attentive guardian and uncle. His growing friendliness was a measure of our good behaviour and acquiescence. Over a quiet drink at the bar on the fifth day, Michel unbent and confided his philosophy to

14

me. This was his fifteenth year on the same run and he knew it all. He had soon learned the hard way the vital need to establish his authority on the first day. Effective management depended upon conformity and punctuality throughout the trip. On the first afternoon of our present tour Michel, clearly, had been true to his precepts.

Our day had started at 08.30 hours at Victoria Station, where reserved compartments awaited us in the boat train. Our main baggage, suitably labelled, was left in the train at Dover, reappearing in the customs hall at Boulogne. This was how it went right through the tour. At each arrival point, mysteriously, the bags turned up outside our bedroom doors, within half-an-hour of reaching the hotel. The next morning, having placed our cases outside our bedroom doors, they would reappear in the evening, at the next port of call, each one at the right door ready to be taken in by its owner.

The organisation, in all its detailed aspects, was masterly. There was no queueing in the reception foyers. We would assemble in a group, all forty of us, to be issued promptly with the cards bearing our room numbers. Each day, while on the move in Europe, we stopped for a morning coffee break, a lunch break and an afternoon tea break. Service at all these cafés was quick, courteous and efficient; the lavatory facilities, bless them, were invariably adequate. Dinner and breakfast at the over-night hotels were equally well managed. All transportation, board, lodging and service having been pre-paid, there were no bills to settle on the mornings of departure, any extras being paid for in cash as we went along.

Sometimes, however, we ate at rather odd hours. Meal vouchers were issued at Victoria to enable us to have

lunch in the cross-Channel steamer. We had to sit down
to this meal at 10.45 hours. On other days, our lunch-
time varied between 11.00 and 14.00 hours. The evening
meal might be at any time from 18.30 hours. I prefer to
draw a veil over breakfast-times, some of which were
truly ghoulish; indeed, the worst feature of our ordeal
was lack of sleep. On five mornings we were roused by
decree within the period 05.30-06.30 hours.

Although the coach seats were comfortable, space
was rather confined and it was difficult to slumber while
travelling; in any case, dozes were subject to the interruption of refreshment stops—and to Michel's frequent
commands. My own seat, being over one of the rear
wheels, was raised higher than the others, but, as its
back was not correspondingly extended, I had nothing
but air on which to rest my head—and, when I sat
upright, my head touched the luggage rack. Some coach
tour operators issue a seating plan in advance, enabling
you to choose your seat at the time of booking. Others
rotate their passengers so that each occupies a different
seat every day. Mine offered no such consolations.

My experience was the more infuriating because, when
booking, I made clear my preference for a seat forward
of the rear wheels and was assured, in writing, that my
wish would be granted. Evidently, the moral is: ask
and thou shalt not receive. On my return I sent in a letter
of complaint; after some delay, I received a handsome
apology, admitting that the clerk had 'looked at the
wrong plan.' So be it.

Among Michel's functions were those of commentator,
interpreter, and purveyor of local excursions. As
Michel's personal interests seemed to be centred
largely on war and women, our notice would be drawn

to every kind of military weapon and emplacement, or to the nubile characteristics of passing females. Matters of cultural, geographical or historical interest were given scant attention. This was a pity. Michel had a willing, camera-armed audience, most members of which would have welcomed more local colour, apart from guns and girls, and a more sensitive commentary on the fleeting scene.

Michel tended also to exploit the merciless broadcast system to exercise his boisterous sense of humour. This tended to be lavatorial, a projection of the lore about public conveniences amassed during his years as a coach guide. I recall his warning on the penultimate afternoon of the trip as we approached Autun, in France. In his execrable English accent, as part of his introduction to the delights of the evening that lay ahead, he divulged, 'In the hotel where we will be staying, there is a room in which Napoleon once slept with Josephine. This is room number six. If any member of our party is allocated this room tonight, take care when looking under the bed for you may find there the original imperial pot, with its royal crown in full colour in the bottom.' Alas, number six was barred to us, and no one got within range of the coveted trophy.

We seemed, in certain respects, an odd mixture. About half our number were over sixty years of age. We were eight Americans, five New Zealanders, four Canadians, two Irish and twenty-one Britons. Michel, being Belgian, and Jean, being French, added spice to the international flavour. For those from far afield, our tour was but one episode in a lengthy trip, embracing several countries. Three of the passengers were semi-cripples, unable to enter and leave the coach without assistance or to walk the streets at our various destinations. Four members of the party, satisfied customers, were doing the same tour for the second time and, clearly, were among Michel's most favoured pupils.

The group comprised mainly married couples. There was one unkempt and painfully shy young bachelor, an ardent coach tourer but, evidently, in the wrong medium for conjugal adventure, there being but three unwed girls among us. One of these, a pretty child of sixteen, was heavily chaperoned by devoted parents. Another, under the close supervision of an aunt, was rather plain and, literally, too bashful for words. The third was an attractive blonde in her early twenties, with twinkling blue eyes and fine legs, but she was paired with a handsome male, somewhat older, and ever at her side. These two, when not talking and laughing together, made jokes and gently teased the rest of us. They were our catalyst of conjecture and, after a week and more of sly observation, opinion was still uncertain about their true relationship; they seemed to occupy separate bedrooms but invariably detached themselves from the group after the evening meal, reappearing together for breakfast the next morning. One hopes, if this was their wish, that the occasion was not without the fulfilment of romance.

The wag of the group was a portly extroverted man in his fifties who, with his quiet wife, occupied part of the back seat and broke into bawdy songs at the least provocation. We had our socially ambitious gossip-monger too, a chirpy and inquisitive lady of uncertain age, accompanied by a lugubrious husband with huge ears. One tweedy gentleman with a military moustache and a delicate wife exercised a constantly roving eye

18

undeterred, apparently, by the poor material at his disposal, but Michel revered him as a tangible link with tanks, howitzers and faded battle honours. There was an elderly man, gaunt and round-shouldered, sweating quietly in a heavy hairy suit, a hill farmer from some remote windswept part of Wales; he was venturing overseas for the first time and looked resignedly bemused throughout the trip.

The Americans tended to keep their own company, conspicuous by plaintive chatter about 'back home', money-changing problems and, yes, the uncertain sanitation of European hotels. Our New Zealanders, affable in a dignified way, would produce maps at the least encouragement to show us the shape and location of their distant country. The Canadians, ever-cordial, were at pains to effect accents and attitudes which, they hoped, would distinguish them from their American fellow-passengers. The Irish pair, spruce, sprightly and quietly gracious, mixed little with the crowd. And we had among us, inevitably, three kindly, anxious, middle-aged spinsters, with bright smiles and sad eyes, hoping wistfully for something to turn up.

On the first day the company seemed colourless, without shape or distinction, but the personalities and characters emerged gradually and, by the ninth day, we were a group of individuals, bound together by our common experience, yet each a separate being with his own identity. We kept to the same coach seats all the way but at every meal sat at different tables among different neighbours. By this means, and through the added experience of local excursions, every member of the party soon became acquainted with all the others. Talk flowed easily on a superficial level, there being a strange lack of curiosity or enquiry about one another's real interests, occupations and family backgrounds. We became well enough aware of our companions' foibles and idiosyncracies but, in retrospect, I can remember almost nothing of substance about these good people among whom I lived in such close contact for several days.

Another remarkable feature is that everyone, throughout the journey, remained even-tempered, cheerful and, apparently, in excellent health. I should have thought that such a trip, for the elderly or delicate, might prove at times to be a fairly considerable strain; the programme was arduous and the chances to recover from weariness or a passing ailment were few. On the other hand we were, in effect, shut off and protected from the rougher edges of the outside world, and it was not too difficult, after the first day, to achieve and maintain a mood of relaxation. For many members of the party, there was also the fact that this tour was a genuinely enthralling experience and, accordingly, a tonic and a stimulus.

Our journey took us to four countries—Belgium, Germany, Switzerland and France. The standard of hotel, food and amenity throughout was commendably high. Service everywhere was friendly and attentive. After the first night, in Brussels, and our afternoon call at Cologne, we had two nights in Germany, the first at a charming riverside spa, called Bad Ems, and the second 4,000 feet up, at Feldberg, a resort in the Black Forest.

Our main Swiss stops were Lucerne and Interlaken; at the latter, where we spent two nights, with accommodation in the delightful Hotel Victoria Jungfrau, we enjoyed the only leisurely break of the trip. This was our 'half-term' holiday and we revelled in it, not least because it offered the most dramatic of the available side-trips, a day out on the Jungfrau by train and lift.

The local excursions elsewhere were more pedestrian. In the larger cities they took the form of a coach tour of the illuminations, or a visit to some of the night clubs; of the latter, the most stimulating was a Swiss evening-out at Lucerne, foaming *steins* of potent beer and community yodelling withal. Most members of the party signed on for virtually all the optional excursions and, whenever Michel recommended a particular shop for souvenir hunting, the party would jostle its way in and faithfully make its purchases. By the end of the trip we were well loaded down with lace, pottery, cuckoo clocks and musical toilet-roll holders.

Unluckily some of the tour's scenic highlights were dimmed by mist and low cloud. But we had a good view of the Rhine's majestic reaches and it was fairly clear as we topped the famous Brunig Pass. We enjoyed some fine panoramas of Swiss lakes and mountains though at Lucerne the great Pilatus was totally obscured. Apart from the overnight stops, we paused for a brief look around several attractive towns and cities, notably Aachen, Heidelberg, Freiburg, Berne and Sens.

The concluding stages of the journey took us through the Burgundy wine country, with Paris as the ultimate highlight. As we sped through the sunlit French country-side on that last full day of road travel, a joyous end-of-term feeling pervaded the coach. We were no longer the timid and bedraggled group which had been marshalled so fiercely at Boulogne; we were now a bunch of confidently naughty children, ever ready under Michel's watchful eye to mend our manners, but otherwise given to puerile jokes and mischievous uproar. For three hours our school wag, from the back seat, led us in full-throated singsong—none of this modern dirge, mind you, but rousing music-hall songs dating from the first world war and the early twenties. When our driver, Jean, pulled out to overtake another vehicle, he would be loudly applauded; sometimes, he would respond cheerfully with toots on his hooter. When we stopped at traffic lights, passers-by would turn and look at us with amazement, wondering if the circus had come to town.

As the outskirts of Paris enveloped us, our guide, thanking us warmly but with a hint of impatience, for our entertainment, counselled moderation and decorum and, finally, silence, while he issued instructions for the last night of term. On this occasion, however, when Michel announced that our call next day would be at 05.30 hours, there were mocking groans of protest and a burst of teasing laughter.

Nevertheless, there we were next morning, after a tame and rather hurried round of cabarets, promptly at 07.25 hours, washed, packed and breakfasted, in our seats, ready for the last lap. Our short night in Paris, of which we expected so much, was a sad disappointment. From Boulogne, after hearty farewells to Michel and Jean, sturdy props of our recent existence, across the Channel and up the smoke to London. The moment of impending release was tinged with sadness; we were about to re-enter our customary world of strife and struggle, the firm protective hand of Michel no longer there to steady and support us. At school, one keeps going with the prospect of the holidays to come but when, at last, anticipation becomes reality, there is often a momentary sense of anticlimax. So it was this time.

Most of us, although glad to be going home, were sorry that our shared ordeal was over.

What had we paid in fees and forfeits? This coach tour had occupied nine days, at an all-inclusive basic price of 42 guineas. This covered all travel from London and back to London, hotel accommodation, main meals and service charges throughout. I found that I could occupy a single room with private bath for a supplementary payment of only 4 guineas; otherwise, anyone travelling alone shared a room with another of the same sex—and this, at the eleventh hour, I funked. Morning coffee, afternoon tea, coffee after meals and all drinks were extra.

If all the local excursions and side-trips had been made, this additional disbursement would have been about £8. We made use of five different currencies, the overall losses on exchange from one to the other amounting to a pound or so. For social reasons it was desirable to offer (or accept) one inexpensive drink at each main meal and this totted up, say, to another £4. Our song-leading wag, inevitably, organised a collection for Michel and Jean, and to this cap we each contributed ten shillings. Thus it might be sensible to assume, if full enjoyment is to be got from a trip of this nature, that the extras, apart from shopping expenses, might add up to between £15 and £20—or approaching 50% over and above the basic cost of the tour.

By any reckoning, it was good value for money. We covered a lot of ground, though never more than 250 miles in one day. There was no night travel. The organisation, the facilities, the service, the condition of the coach and the standard of driving were virtually faultless. We passed through or tarried in a great variety of cities, towns and villages; we enjoyed a fine vista of changing countryside, some of it splendid and magnificent. We had no worries apart from the need to be ready at the appointed time. We went abroad, through four countries, and were none the worse for it.

But, did we? While coach touring is a form of travel, it allows little scope for personal identification with the passing scene. By design, we were insulated from reality, a gaggle of embryos in a cushioned cocoon. Most of what we saw was through glass, as into a television screen. At our hotels, we were small cogs in the vast machine of tourism.

At the end of it all, what remains? A series of hazy impressions, with Michel's broken English as perhaps the only really foreign thing among us; fading memories of laughter and companionship. Coach touring, if not for the adventurous, has its compensations and its stimuli; for those who wish to venture abroad without entirely leaving home it is an ideal form of locomotion. It might well suit Auntie Agatha—but I do not think I would recommend it to her niece.

24

Chapter Two
A Mediterranean Rut

THE brochure of the hotel at Palma showed a handsome
building set back above pleasant grounds with bars, a
swimming-pool and terraces leading down to the edge of
the sea. The idyllic photographs were carefully taken;
there was no sign of any road or other excrescence to mar
the serenity. The reality came as a severe shock.

I was not in an ideal mood for the BEA plane from
London had landed me at Palma Airport nearly three
hours late. The countryside glistened with recent rain
and the sticky heat warned of more to come. A first sight
of the hotel lowered my drooping spirits to zero. The
building fronted on to the main road from Palma to the
west, and this artery divided the hotel from its grounds

and bathing facilities. The connection was an ordinary pedestrian crossing, an arrangement which destroyed any sense of isolation or tranquillity.

Along this four-lane highway, day and night, thunders all manner of speeding vehicle, a constant stream of lorries, buses, cars and motor bikes. It would be quieter and more restful in Piccadilly. The hotel guests, in their sandals and bikinis, wait nervously on the edge of the pavement for a pause in the holocaust, and then scuttle hurriedly, like harassed rabbits, from one sector of their pre-paid facilities to the other.

There can be no more blatant example of the murder of amenity than this relentless road and all that its existence has spewed forth in this continuous, over-developed coastal suburb of Palma, from the Terreno to Cas Catala— the oppressive, featureless, endless cheek-by-jowl hotels and apartment blocks; the dusty, petrol-stenched bars and tea rooms; the shabby souvenir shops; all the tawdry bric-a-brac of modern mass tourism. The objects, or victims, of this grim productive effort, sweating quietly into their crumpled beach-wear, hug the narrow pavements, hemmed in by the merciless traffic, as they make their way from café to bus stop, from *piscina* to lodging house, from wine shop to villa. If this is a typical glimpse of Utopia's age of leisure, heaven help us; a return to the treadmill might be a blessing.

Of course, the environs of Palma are only the beginning. Majorca, as a whole, is a delightful island, endowed with every variety of scenery, from majestic mountains to pine-scented coves and sandy beaches. It has something to offer almost every taste and is favoured with a marvellous climate. It has one main fault; it is too small to accommodate all the hordes pouring into it. All the resort areas, the roads and the public transport are thick with tourists throughout the summer and early autumn and, even in the winter, seclusion can be found only off the beaten track.

The mountains and the less accessible parts of the countryside are peaceful and, in the hinterland of the northern coastline, it is possible, if one can find accommodation, to enjoy an away-from-it-all sojourn among the gentle Majorcans who, despite the constant invasion of their island by sunseeking foreigners, retain their traditional charm and smiling good humour. At heart, they are prouder of the poets, writers and composers who, at various times, have come to live and work among them than they are of the prominence achieved by their land in the world's tourist literature. No doubt the material advantage of being the universal holiday-makers' paradise does not entirely displease them; it is greatly to their credit that they have not been spoiled by it.

My visit to Palma was part of a so-called all-in or two-centre or double-star or two-for-the-price-of-one holiday. The descriptive handle varies with the tour operator. It is still a relatively unusual idea to include two destinations in the same two-week tour, the majority of offerings comprising a fortnight at a single destination. The first stage of my trip was at Palma and the second at Sitges. These two resorts are among the most popular destinations for British package tourists, certainly in Spain, possibly in the Mediterranean as a whole. It should be easy enough to fall into this particular rut but I have seldom had so much difficulty in getting started.

The holiday brochure which I selected, among the many advertising tours of like character, was a gaudy

27

appetite-whetting affair, which happened to come my way, at second hand, through one of the larger retail travel agents. Having earmarked a tour which interested me, I telephoned this agent to ask about the difference in price between certain variations of air and rail travel, and to find out whether the advertised hotels were likely to have accommodation available on the dates I had in mind. The agent said I must pay a deposit before any enquiries could be taken. I saw no reason to part with any money before I knew whether or which of the facilities on offer would suit me but my remonstrances were to no avail. Apart from this, the manner of the gentleman on the telephone was impolite as well as patronising, and it was clear from our discussion that he did not know his way around the brochure as well as I did.

So I decided to cut him out and deal direct with the tour operator. I rang this company's head office, quoted the reference number of the tour I had in mind, and asked whether there were any vacancies. Before I had time even to specify my intended dates, the crotchety lady who took my call snapped: 'The tour you want is fully booked,' and rang off. I tried again, prevailing upon her to listen until I had formulated my request; when she learned that I had an October fortnight in view, she relented. I repeated to her the queries I had made earlier to the travel agent and was given the same shirty reply. 'When you have paid your deposit,' she snapped, 'we will let you know the answers.'

My hide was becoming tougher and I decided to persevere. The brochure offered me the choice of several hotels, both in Palma and in Sitges, and between air travel or travel by rail and sea. I wanted to know whether I could be given a single room in a specified hotel in Palma, and another likewise in Sitges; and what would be the difference in price between air travel by day, instead of by night flight, and, alternatively, surface travel, including sleeping berth on the French overnight train and in the Spanish ship serving Barcelona and Palma, but otherwise second-class all the way. As these travel variations were an option advertised clearly in the brochure, I saw no reason why I could not be told their relative costs before entering into any commitment, however provisional. My caution was due also to a phrase in the operator's brochure, hidden away inside the back cover, which said, 'Should you be obliged to cancel your holiday for any reason whatsoever, the deposit will be considered forfeited . . . and forfeiture of the deposit is applicable whether the booking has been confirmed or not.'

As communication by telephone was not getting me very far, I arranged a personal call at the operator's head office, only to get exactly the same response from an extremely testy and bad-mannered female behind the counter. So, my next move was to complete the operator's official booking form, setting out the alternatives I had in mind.

This document had come with the brochure and, one side of it being dense with small print, took a lot of digesting. After filling in the particulars, and signing in the space provided, I ruled through and initialled two or three of the phrases regarding forfeiture of deposit, the purport of which did not appeal to me, upon which I mailed the form without enclosing a deposit. My form came back to me by the next post with a letter saying, 'We are unable to proceed until we receive a deposit,' followed by the suggestion that I should try again by returning the form, together with my remittance; but I had won a minor victory, for there was no reference to the deleted clauses.

Undaunted, I took up my pen, addressing a letter to the managing director of the company. I was a good deal more restrained than he deserved. Once again, I outlined the information which I sought, and pressed him to supply it before trying to part me from my deposit money. I pointed out how odd it seemed to be expected to make a payment towards the cost of a product, the exact price and colour of which had not been divulged. 'After all,' I went on, 'I might not want to undertake this tour if the price seems too high or if the chosen hotels are not available.'

Two days later I received a crisp but friendly reply, signed on behalf of the managing director. This gave me all the details I needed about comparative prices and implied, though it did not state categorically, that the accommodation which I sought could be made available in the specified hotels. The letter concluded with the offer to proceed upon receipt of my deposit but, craftily, asking for a bigger deposit than that stipulated in the brochure.

I responded by returning the booking form, duly amended in the light of the managing director's letter and of my considered decision to travel outward by day flight and back by night flight. I enclosed a deposit for the lesser amount quoted officially in the brochure and I wrote, 'I assume that this deposit will be returnable in full if you are unable to meet my precise requirements regarding travel and accommodation, or offer me acceptable alternatives.'

From this point, I imagined that all would be plain sailing. I was wrong. Having been sent a receipt for my deposit with the assurance that my arrangements were now in hand, and then having heard nothing for several weeks, I telephoned the tour operator to check that all was well, only to learn that his office had mislaid my papers. But relationships were now on a fairly cordial basis, and, with only two weeks to go before the departure date, the operator leaped into frenzied action. There would be no further hitches. Then, a week later, he rang me. He hoped I would not mind but it turned out that the hotels I had specified in Palma and Sitges were both fully booked; would I please accept particular substitutes of the same category? I would, and I did, for life was now too short for serious argument.

Confirmation of all details, together with the tour operator's itemised bill, reached me five days before I was due to leave London. I sent off my cheque and received tickets, labels and route instructions by return post, despite an assertion in the operator's brochure that, 'Cheques can be accepted only at the latest ten days before departure.' Clearly, I had become a favoured customer. I just about had time to pack and get to the airport.

I cannot blame the operator for the late running of the plane from London, nor for the periodical rain which marked my stay in Palma. It was early October and, between the storms, hot enough to swim by day and drink under the stars by night. Having closed one's eyes and ears to the main road bisecting it, I must say that my hotel was superbly run and had a delightful staff. One was made to feel more like an honoured guest than a package tourist.

31

This hotel was not in the highest category, but nor was it in the lowest; for the money it was, on balance, a good buy. I had sole occupation of a double room with a balcony facing over that road, towards the port of Palma; there was a fine lounge, terraces, a suave little bar and a well-appointed restaurant. The hotel was crammed, largely with Germans, but the meals were served swiftly, and with grace and good humour.

There was a sprinkling of Britons, studiously acquiring their autumn sun tans. Some of the Germans were singular for their girth; one triple-chinned gentleman accompanied by three plain, obediently respectful women, was almost totally round. He ate voraciously including the pickings off his ladies' plates, and was more than an eyeful in the swimming pool, the water level of which would sink visibly whenever he emerged, panting, from the depths. There were several expressionless, quietly-munching, married couples and a party of three single girls, all with identical, elaborately-coiffed structures poised upon their heads. Although their faces changed from white through rosy to brown in the bright sunshine, their hair styles never altered; when they swam, all that showed was three floating beehives and, if they went to bed at night, it was obviously not to lay their heads upon the pillows.

Among the English was one garrulous family from the north, whose relentless object was to collect and corner as many English-speaking acquaintances as they could find; wherever they settled, there was at once created a hearty slice of Anglican pub life. In contrast, there was an aloof couple, led by a tall, unbending man who froze any attempt at familiarity; his gangling and leggy girl, ravishing in body-clinging pyjama suits, was apparently no more able than the rest to warm his ardour.

On my first evening, the local representative of the tour operator had called to welcome his newly-arrived customers and offer assistance. He was a mine of sensible information and of suggestions for local excursions. I went on two outings during my stay in Majorca. One was to the Camp de Mar and intermediate beaches, and the other to Formentor and Alcudia at the far corner of the island. The latter, including a return journey through Soller, involved a dramatic drive over the mountains and along the northern coastline, and provided a surfeit of scenic splendour. The destinations, however, although picturesque and interesting, were swamped with fellow-tourists; at least one could hardly complain of not feeling at home.

On the seventh day, a car came to take me to the airport, where I joined a Spanish plane for Barcelona. Here again a car awaited me, and I was in Sitges within the hour.

It was a day of fiesta and the town swarmed with Spaniards on holiday. In Majorca, the local inhabitants seem to retire into the background but in Catalonia they are not so self-effacing; one is more obviously a visitor in a foreign land, despite the traditions of tourism. Sitges has retained its native charm; the souvenir shops and tea rooms are evident but do not obtrude and, although the narrow streets seem full of predominantly British visitors, the mood and atmosphere are essentially Spanish.

My hotel was on the relatively traffic-free sea front, facing through palm trees to the wide sandy beach. Alas, although ostensibly of the same category as the one in Palma, the appointments of the Sitges hotel were not in the same class; the modern bedroom, with its thin partition walls, reverberated with the din of banging doors, flushing cisterns and grunting neighbours. Again, I had sole use of a double room but it was minute, sparsely furnished and without a balcony. The nearby elevator announced its every arrival with a clang of triumph. The restaurant was a gloomy room, indifferently managed, and adorned with hideous murals. There was a noisy bar, with some easy chairs and tables, and nowhere to read or write in peace. The hotel staff were quite pleasant but the service was perfunctory.

Fortunately, the weather was kind and the hotel saw little of me between meals. On the day after my arrival, the lady representing my tour operator in Sitges arrived to pay her respects and answer questions. My fellow-tourists were mostly from England. It was easier there to break free if one wished to, for one was not confined by the limits of a small, tourist-heavy island.

Sitges is connected to Barcelona by an electric railway and I devoted one day to a tour of that city. On another day, equipped for bathing, with a picnic lunch supplied by the hotel, I took myself to Calafell, a seaside village with a magnificent beach in the direction of Tarragona.

In the evenings, it was pleasant to meander around the streets of Sitges, buy a drink in its bars or take refuge in the sumptuous lounge of a superior hotel close by. One need not want for company for in the hotels and bodegas of Sitges, as of Palma, one's compatriots, idling their fortnight away, are ever-ready to be matey. In October, when Sitges has put up some of its shutters for the winter, its visitors tend to be staid and middle-aged folk, gently-mannered fugitives from trim suburban semis; the talk is cosy rather than scintillating, and the company

34

relaxing. My days and nights sped by fast enough and soon it was time to head for home.

The return journey was by Iberia night flight, with a connecting minibus from Sitges to Barcelona airport laid on, as before, by the tour operator. By midnight, I was back in London, tanned, relaxed, somewhat over-fed— and the poorer by some £100 for my experience.

Of this sum, the tour operator had taken £75 to cover air fares, road transport between foreign airports and hotels and twelve nights' accommodation, with full board and service included; this payment covered also a single room surcharge and a one-way day flight supplement. The price range of my tour, assuming travel by scheduled air services, and depending on the class of selected hotel, was from £50 to £100 approximately— or up to £10 less by chartered air services or second class by rail and sea. This tour operator offered chartered flights three times weekly in the high season, some by day and some by night.

The rest of my money went on payment for local excursions, drinks, essential shopping, tips and incidentals. It was clear that the hotel staffs expected supplementary tips; I was glad to oblige in Palma but I refrained in Sitges. On the whole, despite the poor situation of the first hotel and the scant amenities of the second, my tour was fair value for money. After the difficulties of getting started, the organisation was effective. One had the sense of going abroad independently, though never far from familiar surroundings and helping hands.

Can the truly independent traveller achieve the same object for the same price? I had always thought that a worth-while saving was to be made by buying package holidays. As I discovered by checking and adding up the component prices, I could have bought directly the same accommodation, food and services, and the same flights and road transport, for between £70 and £75—if anything a trifle less than my tour operator's inclusive price. Of course, I would have been denied his local representatives' welcome and, in the high season, due to advance block bookings by tour operators, it might have been difficult to get reservations on the planes or in the hotels of choice. But the answer, generally, is that it pays to shop around and, if little is to be gained financially by buying the best available package, to go independently.

For, although I was well enough cared for, the independent visitor, who is not going to pay his bill until departure, will usually be better treated in the hotels; in the event of disappointment, he can pack his bags, and move on, or go home. One can have too much of Palma and Sitges and, next time, I would opt for a more peaceful hotel in the one and a superior hotel in the other, and stay a shorter time for the same money. Above all, I should be spared all those tiresome arguments and disputes with the tour operator which marred my trip at the beginning. A holiday, like eating out, is meant to be fun—the aperitif as well as the meal itself; and the menu, besides whetting the appetite, should inspire trust and confidence.

Chapter Three
Hard Ways to the Sun

IF you want to travel cheaply, it pays to be a student. In Britain, the NUS (National Union of Students) offers an enticing variety of tours and fares at prices considerably lower than those which the travel trade can offer the public at large.

In 1967, for instance, a student could enjoy fourteen nights at a Costa Brava resort for £37 10s, including rail travel from London, all meals and a shared bedroom in the annexe of a hotel 'within easy walking distance from the beach'. In contrast, one of the largest tour operators in the popular holiday field quoted £44 for thirteen nights all found in a comparable hotel at the same resort, with travel from London by night flight, plus £6 surcharge in the high season. The student could have an eight-day trip to Paris, staying in a youth hostel, for £18 against £34 for the ordinary tourist staying in a simple hotel. Or Sardinia: £46 for a two-week holiday to the student, with accommodation in four-bedded bungalows, or £65 to the ordinary tourist sharing a hotel double bedroom. And Greece: fifteen days in that country, including a side trip by caique to Turkey, for £62, if you were a student, or for £109 if you were a package tourist, though the latter's excursion to Turkey would have been in a fair-sized ship, calling at half a dozen Aegean islands on the way.

The concessions applied also to straightforward travel; for example, whereas the cheapest public night flight return to Rome was £37, a student could get there and back for £27 by air, or for as little as £21 by rail.

These bargains, open to the students of several countries, are the outcome of careful planning by national student organisations which meet together annually to work out their requirements and to share the available facilities. Besides concessions from transport under-takings, the facilities include specially chartered planes and accommodation reserved exclusively for use by students. All you have to do to join a student trip is to present credentials acceptable to the NUS.

In practice, this may not be as difficult as you think. Clearly, a student by definition is any young person studying full-time at a university or technical college but, for student travel purposes, the term includes those who are due to take up full-time studies within six months, or who have completed such studies within two years, and the students' spouses. More interesting, perhaps is the fact that anybody, regardless of age, who has been enrolled for part-time courses at recognised centres of adult education may be eligible for student travel. The listed centres include colleges of arts, housecraft, physical education, horticulture, orthoptics and theology. If the course involves less than twenty hours' study a week, some of the facilities, notably the use of charter planes, are not available but, by and large, most of the concessions can be enjoyed by middle-aged or elderly people who have gone back to school part-time or are pursuing a hobby in their leisure hours through formal study.

But the bulk of customers are young people and one way to judge the value of student tours is to pick one and see what happened to those taking part.

At the time of their story, Joan Harris and Patricia Franklin, in their early twenties, were students at RADA, the Royal Academy of Dramatic Art, in London. Joan, an American, is dark, supple, elegant, with a relaxed manner, masking drive and ambition. Her friend, Patricia, a Londoner, is tall, blonde, vital, with somewhat more panache than the traditional English rose. As this book is meant to be about Britons abroad, it was intended that Joan, remaining off-stage, would merely be the reporter of Patricia's progress but, after their trip, when each produced her own notes about shared experiences, it seemed a pity to miss the chance of dovetailing the two versions into a single and more or less balanced narrative. This is it.

§ PATRICIA: I had never been abroad before. A student tour seemed the right answer, and I knew the NUS tours were well organised and economical. I had friends who had seen the world that way many times. So I went to the nearest NUS office and asked for a booklet. Joan and I chose a three-week tour that would take us first to Turkey and then to Greece. The all-in cost was £70 a head. Our choice took into account that my next term's study was to be Greek drama but we both thought, anyway, that it would be romantic and exciting to see Istanbul and then fly to Athens, hoping that the three-day journey on the train to Istanbul, and the same back again from Athens, would not be too boring. I planned to take a couple of plays to read on the journey to help while away the time.

I went back to the NUS office and joined the end of a gigantic queue of young people clutching booklets and purses and cheque books. When it was my turn, they checked that Joan and I were NUS members; I paid the deposit and was given a receipt and told the itinerary would be mailed to my home within a few days. Then I made off to the Passport Office with my application form, photographs and birth certificate. The man at the desk said my passport would be ready in three weeks; when I told him my holiday started in two weeks he said I could have it the day before I left England. The NUS duly sent me a bundle containing the itinerary, a form called the 'first schedule of information', and a card telling me how to get transit visas for Bulgaria and Yugoslavia. To get the visas I needed my passport, so I rang the Passport Office and they now said I could collect the passport two days before the start of my tour. Having paid the balance owing to the NUS, I went shopping for travellers' cheques and then to get my Isis (International Students' Insurance Service) passport, the cost of cover being 45 shillings.

On the second day before the start of the tour I collected my passport and hurried off to the Bulgarian Embassy where I filled in forms and was asked to return the next morning and be prepared to pay 14 shillings. Next day, the day before my holiday began, I fetched my Bulgarian visa and my passport and jumped on a bus to the Yugoslav Embassy, where I filled in more forms. The man told me to come back that afternoon, which I did, and found there was nothing to pay for this visa and, everything being in order, I set off home to pack and to prepare food for the long train journey across Europe.

I got to Victoria Station with plenty of time in hand. I looked around for Joan and the rest of the NUS party but could find no one. I asked a porter where they were; he said he thought they had already left and I had better see the station master. I rushed to his office, almost crying, and to my horror the station master confirmed that my party had left. I burst into tears. I took out my schedule of information and there it was, 'departure of train 15.00 hours', but the station master said it could not be right for the train had gone out at 14.00 hours. He kindly telephoned the NUS and they said I must go immediately to their office.

Dazed and red-eyed, I arrived at the NUS office where the girl, after seeing my schedule of information, explained that this was only the first schedule and, surely, I had since received the final schedule which gave a revised departure time.

I now remembered receiving the final schedule but, as I had failed to heed an earlier warning that journey times might be changed, the fault was entirely mine. The girl asked me if I still wanted to catch the tour for, if so, there was no time to be lost. A man then spent almost half an hour making arrangements for me to take a plane, costing me £10, from London to Brussels and, from the airport there, a taxi to Brussels Midi Station, costing about 30 shillings, where the train was due to pull in for fifteen minutes. This allowed three-quarters of an hour from arrival at the airport to the railway station; it would be a tight squeeze but the NUS thought it worth trying.

All this I did, and, to my surprise, everything went smoothly; I think the plane must have landed a little early for, after a James Bondish taxi ride, I had to wait nearly half an hour in Brussels for the train.

I was so relieved when it drew in. Like a mad woman I ran up and down the corridors searching for the NUS tour. As I passed one compartment I heard Joan's voice. I dropped my cases and flung open the door, and there was Joan. She could not believe her eyes; she sat with her mouth wide open while I proceeded to tell her of my crazy adventure. In the same compartment were a Pakistani student, and a first year student from Oxford University describing himself as a slightly lesser genius than Newton. I was taken along and introduced to the other members of the tour. There were three Irish girls from Dublin University; a Scottish girl training to be a doctor; a Canadian girl who had studied journalism; a young married couple, the girl supporting her husband as a research assistant while he worked for his science degree at Manchester University; the tour leader, Tony, studying physics; and a girl called Jackie, a teacher of history, who had studied at Oxford and was to become Joan's great friend and mine.

After the bustle of joining the train, I went along to the wash-room. There were three or four people hanging around the door; a girl told me to go back to my compartment and she would let me know when it was my turn. When I got into the wash-room, goodness—how small it was! It had a tiny sink and the water was cold and, when it came to washing my feet, it was almost impossible to keep my balance on one foot while I lifted the other into the water. It was quite a struggle, the floor sopping wet and soap and bits and pieces falling from the sink with the rocking of the train. My next ordeal was the toilet. The conditions were so bad that I really felt sick and I vowed not to use it again, hoping I could hold out until I found a better loo at one or other of the stations.

My first night's sleeping on the train was dreadful and, when we arrived in Munich next morning, I felt rather the worse for wear. But there was time for all my needs and for a bus tour of the city with Joan before continuing our journey in the afternoon. I decided that I could not spend another sleepless night on the train. I asked an attendant if I could move to a compartment with a couchette. He took me along to a helpful Austrian guard who put Joan, Jackie and me together, the extra cost of a couchette all the way to Istanbul being only £2 10s. The rest of that day's journey was very pleasant and our compartment soon became a little home. That night I had a magnificent sleep.

Most of next day was spent looking out of the windows and, when we stopped at Belgrade, a Yugoslav woman came to share our compartment which had four couchette berths. She was very friendly and kept singing to us and stuffing us with food. In the afternoon, at Sofia, we said good-bye to our Yugoslav friend, whose place was quickly taken by another woman going to Istanbul.

We were nearing the end of our packed food and

becoming excited at the prospect of Istanbul. For the second night running, we were woken by officials wanting to see our passports, but were able to sleep late the next morning. At noon, we got ready to hang out of the windows, craning for our first glimpse of the fabulous city.

§ JOAN : Istanbul, at last! Our two Turkish NUS guides were at the station to meet us—a beautiful Byzantine-looking girl, oval-faced and narrow-eyed, and a very charming and personable boy. Both were seniors in secondary school and spoke excellent English. We were gathered together into three taxi cabs, ten-year-old American cars in an advanced state of unplanned obsolescence, and exposed to our first formidable ride through Istanbul. After a cacophonous rendering of horns and shouts and shrieking brakes, we were at our hotel. It was a modern second-class hotel, recently completed. We were quickly organised two to a room and shown where to find the bath and shower.

After getting settled, we met our guides for a coke in the cafeteria to discuss the programme. We began by marking our hotel on the maps of Istanbul handed out to us, thereby gaining a tiny feeling of security. The city tour was cheap and extensive. It covered seven days, including an overnight paid-accommodation trip to Bursa; the cost for the entire tour was about £5. We were to see Topkapi, the Blue Mosque, the Bosphorus, the fortress of Rumeli, Islamic shrines, the Golden Horn, St Sophia, mosaics, mosaics and more mosaics, and, of course, the Grand Bazaar.

Our group, though tired after the train journey, soon became lively with anticipation. We were to start that evening with a folklore festival, sponsored by the Turkish students' organisation, after dinner at a friendly café near the hotel. But we had reckoned without Patricia's mini-skirt, a style new to Istanbul. Furore! Her passage down the busy streets caused a shuddering standstill—even the traffic slowed, a feat normally beyond the powers of Istanbul's police force. Moments of astonished silence were broken by whistles, howls and buzzes. Some passers-by stared, some ogled, some tried to touch. Our own group reacted strangely; a few members seemed embarrassed whilst others became defiant and protective; two of the girls, a bit put out, were drily scornful. Patricia herself was not too happy about the consternation she was causing, but she had to get used to it since all the three dresses she had with her were bona fide 'swinging London' minis.

Our next battle was bus-catching. Istanbul buses stop briefly and infrequently, to be stormed by desperate crowds. The only way to ensure progress into one of them is to cling to the cloth pattern ahead of you and hope. Once aboard, as one of those smiled on by Allah, you peer out triumphantly at those poor mortals nerving themselves to cross from one side of the street to the other, a foray equally dependent on the aid of divine providence. If caught in the middle, one of the thousands of old American taxi cabs may slow down in surprise and let you pass; being in reasonably good shape, unlike these cars, you then stand a fair chance of making the far pavement at a trot.

The following days had a set sequence; sightseeing after breakfast, lunch at the little café, more sightseeing, then dinner. But we spent a few afternoons at the beach as a change from sightseeing. The three Irish girls suffered rather bad sunburn, and the food did not agree with one fellow, but we were mostly a hale and hearty lot. It turned out to be a blessing to have two guides, since the group's interests, particularly at night, were often split and it was almost imperative to go with a guide as few of the locals spoke English or any Romanic language.

One of the more eventful days started with a visit to the Blue Mosque. Patricia, clad in a matching pale blue mini-skirt, was asked to stay outside but, ingeniously, she improvised her cardigan into a side-buttoned, wrap-around skirt and so made it. After lunch, when we visited the Museum of Turkish and Islamic Art, Patricia somehow got left behind. Having spread ourselves in tactical formation over a quarter of a mile of city, hoping to locate her, we gave her up. She turned up at the hotel, rather late, in the best of spirits, as we were about to call the police.

§ PATRICIA : I left the Museum of Turkish and Islamic Art, turned left, went along the road and could not see the crowd anywhere; so I retraced my steps in case they had turned right and gone the other way. But finding no sign of them, I went back into the museum thinking that there must be some Europeans inside who would speak English. The first three people I saw looked English, so I went up to them. To my relief they were English, all right, and one of the men, leaving his girl friend with the other boy, said he would take me back to the hotel. He had a road map of Istanbul. He was a school teacher from Birmingham. All three had hitch-hiked from France to Istanbul; they were going to hitch-hike to Athens, stay there a couple of weeks and then hitch-hike across the Continent to England. We had a struggle finding the way, stopped for a coke, chatted a while and eventually got there. He was very charming; I wondered if he would have been so friendly had we met by chance in England.

§ JOAN : The overnight visit to Bursa was spoilt by oppressive heat. Six of us decided to brave a Turkish bath, and the relaxation and hypnotic luxury of it redeemed the trip for us. Next day, our last in Istanbul, was free to shop in the Grand Bazaar. We chipped in and bought our guides small gifts. Young though they were, they carried out a well organised tour very competently, yet they were quite flexible, always patient and not the least bit officious which, considering they had us on hand almost every minute, was quite remarkable.

On the twelfth day of the tour, after a smooth early morning flight, we arrived in Athens. Astounding contrast; everything was quiet, pastel or dead white, blazing with sun and heat. Our guide, a twenty-two-year-old engineering student, took us by cab, Mercedes Benz this time, to our hotel, second class, but better than the Turkish version, very modern, with inspiring views of the Acropolis. We were sharing three to a room and, once again, there was a bath and shower on each floor. The afternoon was spent in the roof garden writing letters, sun-bathing and sipping cokes from the hotel bar. That evening, after a roof-top dinner, we went to the Acropolis for the well-known *Son et Lumiére* programme, and then for a walk through Plaka, the old section of the city, with a break for lemonade at a pavement café in Constitution Square. Next morning, we set out to see the Acropolis by day. This was followed by an excellent lunch at a downtown restaurant, and an afternoon at leisure. A few of us went to museums and, in the evening, to the Athens Festival to hear a concert by the Leningrad Philharmonic.

Delphi next day was more than worth the four-hour bus ride, not only for the Temple of Apollo but more so because our guide, a born actor, made the experience seem like an improvisation in the living theatre. Back at the hotel for dinner and another free evening.

The next day being free, most of us made our way to one of the beautiful beaches outside Athens. In the evening the entire group went to see Euripides' Helen performed at the oldest amphitheatre in Athens. There followed a planned day of a visit to the International Archaeological Museum in the morning and a trip to the gorgeous Cape Soumon in time for sunset. Dinner at an out-door restaurant on the way back to Athens included typical Greek specialities—*moussaka*, cheese pie, Greek salads, almond desserts. It proved too much for me and I had to skip a folk dance session.

We were at leisure next day until late afternoon, when there was a tour of the nearby port of Piraeus. After dinner, Patricia and I with Jackie, the young history teacher, kept dates with three Belgians we had met the previous evening. We returned to Piraeus and danced until dawn.

We came to in time for the group's farewell lunch in Athens. Patricia and I, who had found a good reason for staying on, saw our party off at the railway station at 16.00 hours, waving profusely until the train was out of sight. Constitution Square was now almost home to us— we went back there for lemonades and to discuss our next steps.

48

§ PATRICIA : We reckoned we had the ideal excuse for remaining awhile in Greece. It all started when Joan, on a shopping spree in Athens, met a friend from back home; the friend said she knew the casting director of a film being made by Michael Cacayonnis, and she thought they were on the look-out for dancers and extras. The introductions made, Joan took me along to audition and, to our joy, Joan was enrolled as a dancer and I as a 'tourist' extra. The location was a fishing village near Delphi. We travelled down by coach and put up at the cheaper of the two hotels in the village. It was very quiet, almost like a ghost town and there was no night life at all. The film people livened it up quite a bit and soon the prices of everything soared higher even than the prices in Athens.

The first day I went to the wardrobe and tried on all sorts of kinky in-the-future costumes. I was told to report again at six the next morning. We were paid each evening, and were then told the following day's programme and who would be wanted. Joan, having worked as an extra in the mornings, rehearsed hard in the fierce heat of the afternoons for the dancing. There were scores of kids from several countries working as extras and dancers. It was fascinating to talk to people in their strange costumes and discover they were at Oxford or training to be nurses or doctors or scientists. They had heard about the film in Athens and most had come down on the off-chance of getting some work. It was great fun at the beginning but it was beginning to lose its charm after a week or so of getting up early in the morning and standing about all day in the hot sun and going over and over the same shot and having to return time and again to exactly the same position as before.

49

I could stay for only two weeks as I had fixed an NUS plane reservation from Athens to London. Joan stayed longer. I had the chance of meeting Colin Blakely, one of the leading men at the National Theatre, whom I admired tremendously, also Tom Courtenay and Sam Wannamaker and a new young star, Ian Ogilvy, who had not long left RADA and, of course, the fiery Michael Cacayonnis. It was a great experience . . .

So ends the girls' story. Both were home in good time for their next term at RADA. The trip had become a bit of a busman's holiday but for Joan and Patricia, dedicated to their profession, it was clearly none the worse for that.

The cheapest buy that I could find for the ordinary non-student citizen with an eye on Greece was a walking tour offered by a British organisation specialising in this type of holiday. My delegate this time was Shirley Fry, an enterprising and attractive lady in her thirties, married with three children, who partners her husband, Cyril, in his art-dealing business.

Neither Fry had previously done a walking tour but they wanted to go to Greece as cheaply as possible, the chosen trip suited their off-season travel dates and the efficiency of the organisers impressed them. The various tours were planned and graded according to the energy or experience of the participants and, while each was open to people of all ages, some care was taken to achieve a balance of interests and of sexes in each party.

Shirley's tour was not one of the most strenuous, to her relief as well as Cyril's. The price of £77 a head all-in included night flight to Athens, four nights in that city in a simple but comfortable hotel, coach transport to the walking area, adequate accommodation in local *tavernas*, a programme of walks and the full-time services of a guide.

There were twenty-four people in the party, all Britons. Their ages ranged from the early twenties to the early sixties. There were four married couples, the rest being bachelors and spinsters travelling alone or in pairs. Civil servants, local government officers and school teachers predominated and seven members of the party were keen botanists. It was a fairly staid group. Shirley, whose skirts are by no means mini, was the only woman to bare her knees. The chief romantic interest was provided by the guide, an English girl in her early thirties, securely trousered, who was pursued throughout the tour by an ardently attentive Greek gentleman.

On the third day of the trip, the party was taken by coach to the Island of Evia, where Propkopian became the centre for five days. The party then transferred on foot to Limni, a fishing village, returning to Athens by coach two days before the return flight.

In Athens there was a minimum of organised outings but, on the island, each day was quite fully planned. The walks varied considerably in distance and in character. As each lasted the best part of the day, picnic lunches were carried. The pace was leisurely. The longest hike covered twenty-five miles and proved a little tougher than the party's experience and stamina warranted; the guide said it was an experiment and she would recommend its exclusion from the low-graded tours in the future.

A typical walk, some ten miles in length, started along the shingle road beside the beach, turned inland, and then climbed steadily up the local mountain to a monastery, from which there were extensive views across the sea and along the mainland coast. The monastery, off the beaten track, was the refuge of an order of cheerful nuns who go about their business on donkeys and, by way of hospitality to occasional callers, endorse their greetings with generous plates of Turkish delight. The return route to the inn ran inland over rough country alive with wild orchids and irises, with a scenic splendour reminiscent of Switzerland.

As patrons of the leading *tavernas* in each of the two village bases, the members of Shirley's party found themselves in the centre of the local social life. The natives, unaccustomed to visitors, were without guile and their hospitality and friendliness without calculation. Much *ouzo* and *retzina* was drunk in the evenings. The guide had brought tapes of Greek dances and English pop music, and there was dancing and singing on most evenings for those wishing to take part. The food was very simple but clean and palatable; there were only two mild cases of stomach upset throughout the trip.

Although some friendships were formed and small groups splintered off according to their common interests, the party as a whole played along together without friction. Shirley and Cyril tended to spend most of the time with a middle-aged town clerk and his wife, one of the few eligible young bachelors in the party and a lonely lady of indeterminable age. The town clerk, an experienced rambler, was accepted tacitly by the party as its leader, not that this entailed any special responsibility.

The chief lack was of shops selling the kind of goods regarded in richer communities as necessities of life, and of drinks and refreshments other than those of local brew. The party in effect went native during its stay on the island and, by common consent, was none the worse for it.

The organisation throughout was thoughtful and intelligent, making allowance for individual whims and inclinations. No one was obliged to attempt feats of endurance and the beginner, or anyone lacking dedication as a rambler, had no cause to feel embarrassed. To Shirley and her husband the trip was a pleasant surprise, good value for money, enjoyable—and likely to be repeated another year.

Well, you may not have to be a student to find a travel bargain, but it still costs you that bit more. And it seems that you must be ready to rough it a little by day—and to sing for your supper at night.

Chapter Four
In Search of Culture

A BOOK about tourism cannot ignore Italy. No country has been longer at the game, yet generations of experience in the role of host have not destroyed the magic of Italian hospitality. The Italians are professionals; a dissatisfied tourist is both bad business and a reflection on cherished and carefully-nurtured skills. But the warm, gregarious nature of these people is what finally gives them the edge over most of their competitors. The visitor is there to enjoy—and to be enjoyed—in a sunny land of infinite beauty and variety.

My wife, Felicity, is an italophile and this, broadly, has been her view of Italy. Always alert for an excuse to go there, she jumped at the chance offered by this book.

E

Yes, she would willingly deputise for me, package tour or not, and her sister would be pleased to accompany her. She succumbed patiently to my careful briefing. Our sitting-room floor became strewn with travel literature. She took her pick and made her plans. This is her story.

§ The agent's brochure of Italian holidays included one which combined the three places of our choice—Venice, Florence, and Rome. One hot day in August we presented ourselves at the agent's head office in London, where an avuncular gentleman beckoned us to draw our stools closer to his counter. We confided our wish to book a slightly adapted form of the preferred tour. The flush of enthusiasm on Mr X's face gave way to a pale look of resignation; pernickety female travellers were evidently his nightmare. We were invited, warily, to state our special requirements.

With our eyes on our waistlines we proposed, for a start, demi-pension terms throughout. Our friend explained patiently that this would almost certainly prove more expensive than full pension, for it would transgress the 'special arrangements' made with the hotels. Hopefully, we suggested bed and breakfast only but quickly retreated on being told what two weary ladies might have to suffer in pursuit of *ad hoc* dinners in a strange country. We then requested single rooms with shared bathroom, naming a hotel in Florence which, unluckily, appeared to offer doubles only. Would it not be more prudent to choose hotels recommended from Mr X's own experience? He now proceeded to describe these in such glowing terms that we had not the heart to persist with our alternatives.

An hour later we had been rendered amenable enough

to part with a £10 deposit, on the assurance that it would be refunded in full were we to decline the official quotation. This arrived the following week, and, triumphant that we had after all achieved demi-pension terms, we accepted the price of £124 per head for a ten-day tour, including air travel to and from Italy by day services. Mr X was clearly disappointed that only I bothered to attend his final briefing, the climax of which was a ticket-preparation ceremony conducted by our friend who played the stamping machine as others would a four-armed bandit. Then, patiently, he took me through the mass of documents—an itinerary carefully typed in duplicate, the travel tickets, hotel vouchers, labels, insurance forms. He checked our passports and travellers' cheques, and then re-checked the lot. A perfectionist, indeed.

The Trident flight by BEA to Venice's new airport on a fine October day was as efficient and punctual as we had been promised. The passport control officer merely laughed when I confessed in halting Italian that I had mislaid my landing card, inferring gallantly that I was, perhaps, lucky not to have lost myself. Outside the building we stepped smartly into a waiting motor launch, which conveyed us ten miles through the lagoon to San Marco past a skyline of fascinating verticals, first of the new oil refinery then of the *campaniles* of Venice itself. We had covered ourselves reluctantly with the tell-tale tour-identifying labels, but, far from being a badge of shame, these proved invaluable in distinguishing us from a group of transatlantic cousins, who were being accorded a markedly lower priority, while ensuring our instant recognition by the couriers. One of these, a charming young man, greeted us by name at the landing place and escorted us the few yards to our hotel right on the Grand Canal.

We had expected a boarding house full of Mr X's but it was only the food that did not surpass our expectations. Our single rooms had a down-alley view of the water which smacked and splashed against the stonework. It was an endless pleasure watching the passing traffic, from gondola to ocean liner, against the background of beautiful buildings. The Venetians, of course, have other interests and I gained an eager, early morning audience in an office opposite my window where watchful eyes played peep-bo round the curtains hoping that the sleeping body would prove to be a sleeping beauty. Later I would get my own back, observing the plump tycoon who, having settled himself at a large desk, began an arduous day—opening letters, reading the newspaper, filing his nails and consulting his diary.

We were enchanted with Venice from the very first evening. It was pure joy to wander free from threatening traffic or spend a leisurely hour in the romantic setting of Piazza San Marco where the crowds stroll to the strains of Viennese waltzes, their admiration divided according to taste between the cathedral with its golden mosaics and the roving pigeons. Venice was to prove the perfect playground for two inconsequent females who, having no plan, were quite content to get lost in the maze of alleys; and who found the climate so relaxing that all they asked was twelve hours undisturbed sleep each day and the certainty that, with clothes and hair bedraggled by the damp, they would disgrace no one of their acquaintance.

We were too idle even to join one of the English-speaking tours which paraded in the square at nine o'clock to file like a school crocodile past one 'important' building after another, bemused by a mass of dates and data. Instead, our days were full of the unexpected as, confounded by the advice to go *siempre diretto* into impassable stone walls, we made our tortuous way to districts entirely different to those we had intended. By chance, we became connoisseurs of churches, some cold and formal, others enlivened by a touch of genius, such as Titian's unforgettable painting of the Assumption over the altar in the church of the Frari; and we returned again and again to the basilica of San Marco, with its wonderful atmosphere reminiscent of Pope John. Our memories of dark Italian museums and even darker paintings made us shy of the Accademia until nearly the end of our stay, when we regretted our ignorance of this profusion of Venetian colour. Below, for a shilling cup of *cappochino*, we could enjoy a perfect view of the Grand Canal, and thence take a boat back to San Marco.

Then there was the Biennale, a word that has such a delightful ring. We joined other visitors who had come to Italy specially to see the selected exhibits of modern art set unobtrusively in Venice's only park. Avoiding a pile of silver baubles which looked as though they had fallen off a giant Christmas tree, we made our way to the French pavilion.

There used to be a party game where a mass of objects were piled on top of one another, the winner being the child who could afterwards recall the greatest number. I was never much good at this but here I was able to remember the collection attributed to a certain Etienne Martin that looked like a porter's trolley draped with matting, curtain cords and brass trinkets, and was itself a prize-winning exhibit. In the next room, a female face with neon lips peered down from the wall, driving us and a surprisingly fast-moving party of priests to take refuge elsewhere. Gaining scant consolation in the British pavilion next door, we turned into that of the United States which offered some smashing colour samples; and then to the German pavilion with the prizewinning paintings of grotesque bodies by Horst Antes. Most of the exhibits, like advertisements, were designed to make immediate impact, so we felt no guilt at responding to them in record time. It was a great relief to priest and heretic alike when the final pavilion turned out to be the restaurant.

We spent our last afternoon attending to the more subtle touches of Byzantium and the Doge's Palace, whose pink and white marble must have made it a real bobby-dazzler in its early days. We gazed at the beauty of its ceilings until our necks felt as distorted as some of the figures in the Biennale. Then, at sunset, we took a lift to the top of the Campanile and tried to restore the balance of our bodies, looking down at the lagoon bathed in its strange melancholy in the pink mist.

We had only barely begun to discover the endless variety of Venice when the gondola arrived to take us away. Mr X had arranged that we should leave in style but had not foreseen the adventure of a departure on a windy day, when the hurrying assortment of motor boats turns the Grand Canal into a splashing cauldron. Despite the skill of our gondolier, we sampled the waters more than once, disembarking at the station in an even moister state than usual. We were greeted there by another representative of our agency whose charm did not compensate for the absence of seat reservations on the *rapido* to Florence; Mr X had assured us that these would await us at our hotel and our hotel had assured us that they would be at the station. As the train was fully booked we had to hope for an empty seat in the carriage coming through from Trieste, or settle for the ordinary express which offered no lunch and added two hours to the journey.

Few Italians can match the dogged skill of an English-woman in the art of queue-jumping, and we managed to get the last two seats in the *rapido*, the worst-run train I have ever known. All was total confusion, with people stacked in the gangway surrounded by their babies and baggage. Our tempers were not improved at Florence where the courier walked us in circles in search of his favourite taxi, the taxi then proceeding in circles because of one-way streets and traffic blocks. By the time we had found our rooms in what looked to be the servants' quarters of the hotel, we wished only to circle right back to Venice, with its timeless tranquillity.

Having been unable to buy lunch on the train, we now set out in search of victuals. A bottle of local wine and a dish of *tagliatelli* in the Piazza Santa Maria Novella worked wonders for our morale, but to our jaundiced eyes the centre of Florence looked like Manchester or any other pedestrians' purgatory on a dismal Saturday afternoon. It turned out to be British week, with St Michael's ware in every window, a Whitbread pub in the main square and a band of Highlanders adorned with bagpipes. We fled towards the Arno where the little riverside shops were full of those tortoiseshell and onyx ornaments that are never shown to such advantage back in England and then threaded our way back through endless hooting cars to take refuge at the hotel hair-dresser. For him, Florence had a long way to go before it could rival London, the mecca, where he could change his work every week and his girl friend every night.

Prosperous though Italy had become, there were none too many jobs—and far too many omnipresent mothers.

In Venice there had been the welcome of Harry's Bar at the end of the day. Now, resplendent with an Italian hairstyle, we decided to promote ourselves to Florence's best hotel for a *negroni*. It was palatial but, as it appeared to be running an American week, we retired to our more modest abode, to find it had attracted a bus load of ladies, their breasts labelled *ON THE GO*, with such further marks of distinction as *Iris from Dakota* and *Lily from Alabama*, all rather reminiscent of a showground. The dinner was a set one to suit the influx of customers. After we had noted the mastication it required, we rejected the steak—also the chips and the ice cream and fruit salad—and pressed for an Italian menu instead. This caused a bit of a flurry but we managed in the end to browbeat the head waiter into speaking his own language and providing us with a very good dinner.

Next morning the American tour, living up to its name, could be seen following its leader into the pouring rain. The Uffizi gallery was pleased to receive us but, by midday, we could hardly move in it. Some of the cars, at least, were having a Sunday at rest, enabling us to recapture the real flavour of Florence as we wandered round its lovely squares and churches. In the afternoon we took a bus to Fiesole, which I remembered as a deserted village one winter's day in 1950; while nothing could ruin its superb view of Florence, the simple square, which once had its own magic, was now virtually a car park.

We were not too sorry to leave Florence next day, when a minibus collected us at eight to join the coach to

Rome. The coach depot was extremely efficient and, despite torrential rain, our journey was enjoyable. A delightful hostess gave us the minimum of information over the loud speaker system, chatting thereafter to any passenger who wanted more. Our first break was at Arezzo, a splendid hill town with a beautiful square as yet untouched by progress, and we had time to see the colourful frescoes of Piero della Francesca in the church of San Francesco. Mr X had supplied us, unasked, with vouchers worth 1,800 lire each for lunch in the large hotel in Perugia, the main stop. One look in the gloomy dining room, featuring hamburger, fried egg and chips as a star dish, decided us to brave the deluge, our reward being a small Italian restaurant which produced excellent *tagliatelli a la perugiana*, red wine and coffee for 800 lire each. Perugia, with its heavy architecture, felt like a northern fortress. The low cloud blotted out the plain below but we could see how the city is spreading its tentacles towards the shores of the lovely lake Trasimeno, where a summer bathing resort is being developed. A huge chocolate factory contributes to its prosperity, and the narrow roads already have their fill of traffic.

After descending from Perugia, physically replete, we ascended in every sense to Assisi. The town was shrouded in mist, emphasising the stillness of the basilica of San Francesco. A coldly efficient English friar conducted us smartly round its two churches, intoning his obvious preference for the upper Gothic structure with its famous frescoes by Giotto. We were behind schedule and another coach load was awaiting his services, but not even the ignominy of our status could mar the atmosphere of peace and the sense of wonder that all this magnificence had been created in the thirteenth century,

63

one whole church having been built by hand within two years—a real labour of love.

We rejoined the bus in company with an extra passenger, an Assisi wasp, which aroused the murderous instincts of all but the true followers of St Francis, reducing us to a state of consternation. The hero of the hour was our driver who managed to capture the intruder with the help of our *Sunday Express* and return it to freedom, thus satisfying the honour of both factions. Our journey continued in the ever-pouring rain across the Appenines to Terni, a town largely rebuilt since the war which does little credit to present day architects. A wretchedly narrow road then took us past the famed blue rivers of the Neri and we climbed a ridge, where the trees were festooned with vines, before rejoining the *autostrada*, upon which the weather cleared miraculously to reveal a red sunset.

As darkness fell we were approaching Rome—a time of great emotion for our ancestors who had braved bandits, bedbugs and bumps to reach the target of their Grand Tour. For us, it was an anticlimax to arrive at the outskirts and become engulfed in the traffic jam of workers leaving the factories. Our transport, however, was efficient to the last and, once through the garden of the Villa Borghese, the coach stopped in mid-road, within skipping distance of the doorstep of our hotel above the Spanish steps.

We could hardly expect a hero's welcome on being deposited with our baggage in one of Rome's smarter hotels at the busiest hour of the evening, and it was clearly no recommendation to be the bearers of pre-paid vouchers for our stay. We were told curtly that we must make do with a suite consisting of double bedroom, small room with divan, and shared bathroom, as no single rooms were available. The key was handed over and we were left to find our own way upstairs. Flinging open the French windows in fury, we were mollified by the discovery that there was a balcony with a glimpse of St Peter's, not to mention a bird's view of the unending traffic block below. After the church bells of Venice and Florence, we could now hear only the angry hoots of imprisoned cars.

Fear of demotion to a lower floor stilled our complaints though the dinner of tinned hors d'oeuvres, tough tongue and antique cake offered further provocation. Later, the suave maître d'hôted took mercy on us and, for the rest of our stay, we were privileged guests in the restaurant, preserved from tour-party fare, while the hotel bar gave us a rare taste of gracious living with its elegant décor and friendly service.

Our first day in Rome was not a success. Persecuted by traffic even in the narrowest streets, inhaling diesel fumes and exposed everywhere to fellow tourists, we felt only irritation. Piazza Barberini, described in our guide book as the haunt of artists, appeared to be a mere hub for the many wheels, while the beautiful Fontana di Trevi was being cleaned out, reminding us of the same activity in London's Zoo. The Colosseum looked overrun by ants as the endless coachloads of trippers posed for photographs against its walls, their minds, if not their eyes, on the hovering ice cream cart.

Yet, after three days, the same scenes were beginning to regain their magic. Obsessed by the beauty of the old buildings, and enchanted by the quality of the light, we became impervious to the traffic. The churches, which struck us at first as cold and over-ornate, seemed later to present the perfect setting for grand opera. It was like the answer to a prayer when, unexpectedly, a burst from the organ heralded our arrival in the church of Santa Agnese al Circo Agonale in the Piazza Navone, the finest square in Rome. As time went on, pleasant surprises were increasingly our lot. One afternoon we joined a crowd in the Piazza del Quirinale to watch something rather akin to the first act of a provincial tattoo, as three motor cyclists of the *carabinieri* revved their engines before leading the President's ceremonial guard from his palace to the barracks below. Later, we found ourselves on a film set in the Piazza di Spagna, a scene of romantic splendour under the stars, with the church of Trinita dei Monti floodlit above; and, under the arc lights, a beautiful blonde fighting a fiery brunette for the heart of a nonchalant young man in an Alfa Romeo.

CIT offer an efficient service of tours in and around Rome, with a minibus collecting passengers from the hotels before sorting out the nationalities at the Piazza de la Republica terminus. We chose to go to Tivoli in the English-American coach, which was shared with a sprinkling of Japanese and English-speaking Germans. It was a disappointing journey through dull suburbs, across the flat *campagna*, to the Villa Adriana which has the same remote and vaguely disturbing feeling as the Palatine Hill above Rome's forum.

I was retracing the steps of an ancestor who, in 1783, filled an album with sketches of this most magnificent of all imperial villas. He would have been impressed by the zeal, if not the skill, of our party with their whirring cameras, the wives in brisk charge of the operations, except in the case of the more fortunate two-camera couples who could shoot each other almost simultaneously against the second-century pillars.

At our next stop, the Villa d'Este, the steep slopes, damp from the ever-playing fountains, were lined with exhausted pilgrims panting in search of a viewpoint. The Renaissance villa is little more than a shell so, before returning to Rome, our guide released us for a twenty-minute fling in Rivoli itself, which was able to satisfy the most insatiable craving for souvenirs and coffee.

After this rather harassing excursion, we decided to go independently to the Alban Hills, taking a bus to Genzano which overlooks a peaceful lake. Here, for the first time, we were back in the old Italy, with that strange mixture of beauty and squalor which has its own unique flavour. As in Russia, the Communist newspaper was displayed in the town centre, where we caught a bus back to Ariccia, another picturesque town on the same ridge offering wonderful views over the *campagna*. The only restaurant being closed, we hired a taxi to take us along the Galleria di Sopra, so often painted by J. R. Cozens, to Castel Gandolfo where the Pope has his summer palace above lake Albano, with its steeply wooded slopes and the towering Monte Cavo on the far side. Here, in perfect peace, we found a delightful terrace restaurant, where we were greeted like long-lost friends. A special dish of *canneloni* was prepared as we happily drank our way through a large carafe of Frascati white wine. After lunch, we were lucky to pick up a bus to Frascati itself, a pleasant town surrounded by rich villas, its main square dominated by the church where the Old Pretender lies.

Having found our feet, there was no end to our enjoyment—the Villa Borghese with its marbled halls and wonderful paintings; the National Gallery in the

Palazzo Barberini, the ceiling of its great hall a miraculous work by Pietro da Cortona; more paintings in the Corsini Palace and in the Villa Farnesina, both with lovely gardens. The list seemed inexhaustible; we could hardly ignore the Vatican, a day's work in itself, not to mention St Peter's, where English visitors once made themselves so much at home that their talk disrupted the Sunday services.

The Italians are efficient hosts to their countless visitors. Nowhere were we pestered by touts or beggars. Ten per cent service was on the hotel or restaurant bill, the waiters smiling the parting guests through the door with or without further reward. The tour guides dispensed concentrated doses of culture and seemed as anxious as their passengers to leave the coach at the end without tangible thanks. The priests and congregations participating at mass appeared to have superhuman concentration in the presence of constantly shuffling sightseers. But, at the end of the day, most remarkable was the stamina of all those eager tourists, many of them well past their half-century setting out on their marathon evening of bright lights and cabarets.

We were thankful that our tour, although packaged and in most essentials pre-paid, was unescorted, leaving us largely to our own devices, apart from the need to stick to the overall programme and itinerary. We could have done without the privilege (and expense) of being met at our destinations and of having our departures organised. We regretted the demi-pension terms, which involved us in one monotonous hotel meal each day, valued at about two pounds, compared with our excellent one-course 'free-lance' lunches which cost us from ten to fifteen shillings a time, wine and coffee included. It proved a disappointment to find ourselves booked in hotels reserved virtually for fellow-foreigners, mostly female, whose appetite for things Italian ranged from the timid to the indiscriminately voracious. The most demanding of them had their own guide and hire car in constant attendance while others, judging by an *Il Tempo* advertisement 'Rich American women willing marry Italians', seemed to be there with more permanent arrangements in view.

On our last day, which came all too soon, we departed in style, by car to the airport and by Trident, on time, to London. All that remained was to torment Mr X with the saga of our lost seat reservations on the train from Venice, our demand for a refund on the unused lunch vouchers, and our complaint that we had to pay extra for our transport from Venice airport to the hotel. This was the cue for Mr X to assume his most confidential manner and to refer us patiently to the alarmingly long list of notes, in miniscule print, which had accompanied his original quotation. Fearful that the objects of his careful search might be lurking nearer to clause Z than to clause A, we crept quietly out and left him to it.

Chapter Five
Home from Home

AFTER starting this book, I was asked by another publisher to write one about Malta; as some of the research could be done only on the spot, a visit proved necessary. I decided that two birds could be killed with the one stone of a package tour whereby, for the all-in price, one travels to and from by air and, whilst there, enjoys exclusive use of a furnished villa and a self-drive car.

I have been to Malta several times during the past twenty-five years, and much has changed since I first went there. The old colony has become an independent country within the Commonwealth. Goats no longer deliver their milk to the housewives' front doors. Those poorer families who lived in cliff-side caves are decently housed. Around Valetta, the *dghajsas*, ferry-boats, carts and *karrozzins* are slowly going out of business. The great harbours, once the scene of British naval might and pageantry, are given up mainly to yachts and unobtrusive commerce. In the streets, civilians and tourists hold sway where servicemen roamed. The war left cruel scars; while most have been erased, a few still show and all are well remembered.

Yet there is an enduring quality about these islands, with their distinctive character and their long history of battle, occupation and assimilation. The Maltese are a proud people, religious, closely-knit, self-assured; when their affections are engaged they display rare gifts of courtesy and hospitality. Fortunately, they hold their most recent masters, the British, in good regard. After playing host so often to the foreigner, reluctantly or not, the Maltese are taking in their stride the latest invasion— by tourists. They seem to be tackling with verve and sensitivity the creation of amenities to satisfy the needs and appetites of tourism without spoiling the beauty and character of a small and crowded country.

The main island of Malta is only seventeen miles long and nine miles wide; with its sister islands of Gozo and Comino it supports a population of nearly 350,000 people. The airborne visitor's first impression is of a compact land, of spreading towns and villages separated by narrow belts of terraced countryside, the whole set neatly in the blue Mediterranean. The airport is virtually within the Valetta—Sliema connurbation, and the views from the road into the capital certainly suggest a scarcity of elbow room. But everything in Malta is to scale and, after a while, Valetta, with its fine squares and elegant buildings, assumes the majesty of a major city in a large country.

This effect is enhanced in Malta at large by the dignified urban atmosphere of small but self-sufficient villages, dominated by sumptuous twin-towered churches. Their streets, as the rural roads connecting them, twist and turn and meander without apparent logic and, due to a dearth of sign-posting, it is not unusual when attempting to drive through Maltese towns to emerge from them unwittingly from the side at which they were entered. Thus, a journey of a dozen miles in Malta may leave the motorist with the impression that he has travelled three or four times as far; to complicate matters, the inhabitants, who are genuinely parochial, often find difficulty in directing a visitor from one village to the next.

If he is persistent, however, the motorist will soon discover in the northern half of the main island, and in Gozo, a surprising variety and extent of landscape; an abundance of rocky agricultural land and wild looking terrain; dramatic coastal scenery; and a true sense of peace and isolation. Yet those who seek a lazy beach-combing existence may be disappointed; the chief lack in Malta, apart from the ability to penetrate an endless hinterland, is of sandy beaches. Those that exist are barely enough for the Maltese themselves and, at weekends, the seaside resorts are overcrowded. But many of the new hotels are designed as self-contained units, with their own swimming pools, shops and night life and, in the hot season, the customer may not wish to venture very far beyond the perimeter. Exuberant or restless people, young or old, may suffer a little from claustrophobia. But the off-season is another matter.

Then, there is room to move around and to be energetic, without being drowned in perspiration. Having experienced Malta in the hottest months, my own preference is early spring or late autumn.

Before planning my package tour, which was to start towards the end of February, I consulted the brochures of half a dozen London agencies offering villa holidays in Malta. It can be cold there at this season but three of the agencies seemed unaware of this and did not know whether their villas could be heated. That left three agencies in the running.

I rang the one at the top of my list and the girl who answered told me they had no information beyond that given in their brochure. As the brochure said nothing about heating, I pressed her on this question. She went off to consult a file but, drawing a blank, spoke to a friend sitting near her in the office who said that portable room heaters could no doubt be made available. When I enquired about linen there was more muttered conversation, but no one knew whether bath towels were provided. Several minutes having been spent on these simple enquiries, I asked if the details could be sought and sent to me and, meanwhile, could I know whether a particular villa was free for the fortnight I had in mind? I was told all this would involve writing to Malta, and I must first pay a deposit of £5. The brochure of this agency proclaims proudly both its great knowledge of Malta and its pre-eminent position as a villa-letting organisation, but the ignorance of the staff depressed me and I saw no reason to part with £5 in that quarter.

My call to the second agency on the short-list was answered by a taciturn woman who, after persuasion, agreed without charge to get the extra information and ring me back. I heard no more.

The third agency was efficient. A courteous man dealt promptly and explicitly with all my questions but, unfortunately, when it came to the crunch, the choice of properties in the winter was not nearly as wide as the brochure implied and I could not be offered what I wanted. With reluctance, I removed this agency from my list.

It was now necessary to extend my enquiries and these embraced another very helpful firm which, unfortunately could not meet my exact needs. Finally, I came upon a brochure of the agency which eventually fixed me up. This brochure was the best presented of all, offering at all seasons a fair choice of villas in several parts of Malta. Having marked the one I liked most, I rang up. A very pleasant and competent girl, besides answering my questions in a way that inspired confidence, volunteered extra details which demonstrated personal knowledge of the property. She was able to tell me that heating would be by means of electric fires, that all linen except bath towels would be provided, that there were shops within fifty yards, that the villa's main balcony enjoyed sunshine from mid-morning to mid-afternoon, and that it was definitely available on the required dates.

I duly completed the booking form, specifying that enough electric fires should be provided to warm simultaneously all the living and bedrooms, and that I would need a car of a certain size and make. I enclosed with this a deposit of £30 and, within a few days, received confirmatory acknowledgement. This was hardly in my hands when the managing director of the agency telephoned me to suggest that, while he thought my choice of villa interesting, he felt I could do better with one of the others in the brochure. We had a friendly talk weighing the pros and cons, at the end of which I decided to take his advice. The villa he recommended was on higher ground, had a better view, enjoyed more sun and had a telephone line. The accommodation comprised a flat on the top floor of a three-story house and, according to the brochure, was 'of exceptionally high standard'. I was asked for a further deposit of £20 for the telephone which, I was assured, would be connected in time for my arrival.

I sent off a cheque for the balance owing. The total cost, including hire of the flat, hire of car with comprehensive insurance (and no mileage limit), compulsory holiday insurance and return air fare by day flights, the whole covering two weeks, amounted to £199 on the basis of, say, two people occupying a flat for five, that is about £100 each. This figure included inventory and telephone deposits, totalling thirty pounds. returnable at the end of the trip upon clearance of the inventory form and telephone account. The tickets, when they reached me, were accompanied by clear instructions, including information about the duties of the maid and the cheering assurance that the agent's local representative would render all assistance in case of difficulty. He would in any case meet me at the airport, guide me to the villa and make sure personally that I was comfortably installed. He would even be happy to arrange for any provisions to await me on arrival at the villa if I would let him know my needs in advance.

The BEA Comet ran to time. It was nearly full, mostly of middle-aged or elderly people seeking winter warmth and sunshine. They were well rewarded. The temperature at London airport was 45°F and in Malta 63°F. The sun in Malta was bright and fairly strong but the wind was fresh.

At Luqa, the island's airport, the plane draws up close to the visitors' balcony. There is always a cheerful crowd to greet arrivals. The airport is efficient but has a pleasant air of informality. At the exit, the agent's representative made himself known. He handed over the car that was to be mine for the fortnight. Then he entered his own car and drove off slowly, beckoning me to follow. Half an hour later we were at St Paul's Bay. The route seemed easy enough but it needed four subsequent journeys on my own to learn it.

The village at St Paul's Bay is not typical of Malta —no church dominates it and the long narrow high street is more or less straight. We followed the road around the head of the bay and started the ascent of Xemxija (pronounced Shemshiya) Hill. This was the location of my flat. It faced south-east across the bay towards the village. Terraced hills provided a background to the view and the open sea lay over to the left. It was a gorgeous vista and the light on the honey-coloured stone buildings and cottages of the village, particularly towards sunset, was beautiful.

The apartment had a balcony on three sides and shared the use of a flat roof. There was a large L-shaped living-room, furnished generously with sofas, armchairs, a dining-table and sideboards. It sported also an unnecessary bar of revolting design. Some of the ornaments were garish, but I became quite attached to all the abracadabra after a while. There were two bedrooms and a divan behind a curtain at one end of the living-room. The pillows and mattresses were rather lumpy. The villa had not been in use since the autumn, and the bedding was definitely damp. There was a clean, well-equipped kitchen, with an electric refrigerator and a gas cooker fed by cylinders. The food and stores I had ordered were neatly stowed away. Hot water in the kitchen and the bathroom was by means of an Ascot-type heater. The bathroom was a gloomy little room, poorly lit, with a minute mirror.

Our arrival was greeted with a riot of noise caused by cement mixers, bulldozers and other road-making equipment. The street giving access to the villa was being widened. My heart sank—I had not come all the way from London for this. The agent's representative soothed me by taking me to the far side of the villa to show me the view and to prove that the row could hardly be heard in the living-room. As it turned out, the road gangs worked a short day and, on some days, did not appear at all. Only one electric heater had been provided in the flat. The representative, eager to please, ferreted around and produced another three. On the question of the telephone he had to admit defeat. The line was connected to the flat, yes, but the authorities required nine months' notice to bring it to life. However, the representative kindly offered to take messages at his office, a mile away in the village, and to allow me the use of his own telephone.

Having checked the inventory and been paid for the provisions, the representative withdrew. It was now late afternoon and, after unpacking, I went out on reconnaissance. My first find two hundred yards down the road was a small hotel, the Fondatore. Its exterior was unpretentious, but the owners and staff were friendly and obliging and, as I was to discover, the quality of food and the atmosphere in that charming little hotel were quite exceptional. Here again, a message-taking service was offered together with the use of a telephone.

In the main village, around the bay, strung along the high street, was a variety of shops, well able to minister to visitors' needs. The range of goods on sale were similar to those found in a village store in England, but cheaper. The bread, fruit and vegetables were superior and the excellence of the local wines was a constant temptation. There were also two inviting restaurants, one of them built out over the sea in a superb position. I was greeted everywhere with welcoming smiles. The maid, who turned up each morning at nine, was always smiling too. She was happy to turn her hand to any chore short of cooking; washing floors and clothes and dishes was apparently her idea of bliss. Service to the customer in Malta really seems to be a pleasure.

I had plenty to occupy me during my stay, interviewing people and researching for my new book. This activity included excursions such as any tourist with a car would probably undertake.

My first outing took me to the town of Mellieha. This stands on high ground, falling away on both sides into ravines, the whole dominated by a large twin-towered church. A feature of Mellieha is its terraced districts but most dramatic is the view northward across the sea to the island of Gozo. In the foreground, just below the town, is one of the main island's most attractive sandy beaches, Mellieha being almost unique among Maltese towns in having this amenity right on its doorstep. Near by is one of Malta's leading hotels, the Selmun Palace, a converted castle, with a large swimming pool and panoramic views. Its hill-top position is remote and tranquil and the interior has been skilfully treated to provide an ambience of cosy luxury.

My next round started with another look at one of Malta's popular beaches, Ghan Tuffieha, dominated by a rather ornate modern hotel. From there, I took a series of winding country roads over the hills, along peaceful valleys, through the typical Maltese town of Mgarr, and so to Rabat and Mdina. The latter, the former capital of Malta, is a gem of a small walled city, virtually free of road traffic, whose characteristic, apart from fine houses and a superb cathedral, is silence. Here, in quiet seclusion, remote from the modern world, live some of Malta's noble families.

The glory of this city tends to overshadow Rabat, lying on its outskirts. Rabat, in contrast, is a lively and gregarious community whose winding streets have an Arabic atmosphere and contain many historic buildings. Like Mdina, it stands on high ground and enjoys sweeping views over the island.

Another outing included a call at Dingli on the west side of the main island, and a walk along the towering Dingli cliffs. The return journey to St Paul's Bay was by an inland road through Mosta, distinguished for its colourful circular church boasting one of Europe's biggest domes. I went the rounds also of several towns and villages in the centre of the main island—Attard, Lija, Balzan, Qormi, Zebbug and Siggiewi—each of which has an identity of its own. I included, as any tour should, a visit to the St Anton gardens and to the smart Corinthia restaurant.

In the southern part of the main island is a further assortment of communities, outwardly familiar, but the people here have a distinctive regional mood and character, as though their neighbours a few miles to the north were a different species. The south of Malta is destined to become of increasing importance commercially and industrially and may tend to lose some of its attractions to the tourist.

Between the main island of Malta and Gozo lies the islet of Comino with its first-class hotel, a centre for water sports and for a good life away from the motoring crowds. This islet can be reached only by hydrofoil from Valetta or by tender from Marfa, the Gozo ferry's departure point at the north of the main island.

Gozo, the so-called Calypso isle, has been fairly late in the running for tourism but some good small hotels are emerging. This island, mainly agricultural, seems to belong to another century. Its industrious people give the impression that time hardly matters; that, though life is often hard, the Lord in the end will provide. Gozo is a perfect haven for those seeking an escape from today's raucous world.

There are two roads from St Paul's Bay to Valetta. One goes inland through Mosta, while the other follows the coast to the residential town of Sliema, and thence around the harbour creeks to the island's capital. This is a wide new road, and quite free of traffic except at week-ends. In the Sliema area, notably in the vicinity of the Dragonara Casino, the Hilton and Sheraton groups, among others, have opened stylish seaside hotels. Sliema has long boasted a number of good family hotels; among the newer ones the Fortina, facing across the water towards Valetta, is specially inviting.

Valetta, which I visited several times, is one of the world's dramatic cities. It was built to resist invasion on the top of a great rocky promontory, contained within protecting ramparts, and it was one of the first cities to be planned comprehensively with a pattern of straight parallel streets. Some of these end in steep inclines or broad steps and at the extremities are glimpses of the blue waters of the splendid natural harbours, a chief cause of Malta's traditional importance in Mediterranean strategy. The Knights of Malta, in whose time Valetta was created, bequeathed a super-abundance of fine buildings; even to the most persistent sightseer, its charms and fascination are endless.

But Valetta is not too well endowed with hotels and restaurants of international standard. The famous Phoenicia hotel, on the city's outskirts, has recently lost the monopoly which it so long enjoyed, the advent close by of the new Excelsior adding an important amenity for visitors to the Maltese capital.

After ten days, far from seeking items to add to my programme, it became a question of elimination. Not that it is easy to keep to a programme—the weather off-season can be tiresome, interruption of the inter-island ferry service may cause an enforced stay on Gozo, interviews and discussions expected to last an hour or two may well use up half a day. Apart from these, a puncture and some damage to the car caused by a lady reversing into one of its rear lights, my fortnight was free of untoward incidents. There was not even one broken cup to mar the villa's inventory.

Whilst in Malta, I had a quick look at other flats and villas of similar size and character. Hire charges varied considerably. At one end of the scale, the local price of a comparable villa with comprehensively-insured hire car included, for two weeks, came to £90 at off-season rates; at the other end, only £60. At the lower rate, adding the cost of individually purchased tourist return day tickets by air, it might be cheaper to deal direct with the air line and with the local villa agent than to make in London an all-in package deal like mine. But a package tour would be cheaper than the more expensive local arrangement. The permutations vary with the size of the party.

The package tour, obviously, has the advantage of a worry-free transaction. The price reflects the concession rate for the air ticket, but against this must be set the profits and overheads of a London-based agency. Hence the small difference in cost for the customer. As it is usually better to hire a villa which one has inspected personally, there is much to be said for dealing direct with the local agent. But, for those venturing into unfamiliar territory, the kind of all-in service provided for me on my trip is preferable.

The return Comet ran true to form. My fellow passengers looked browner and, perhaps, a little plumper; those who had seemed elderly on the outward journey were now middle-aged and the middle-aged younger. I trust the same could be said for me.

Chapter Six
Invitation to a Ski Party

SHORTLY after I began work on this book, the Wilson government decreed that the Briton venturing on holiday outside the Sterling area must limit his annual foreign spending to £50, plus £15 a trip for travel expenses. This niggling measure, inhibiting the ordinary man's freedom to travel at will and to spend spontaneously on simple pleasures whilst abroad, led me with reluctant patriotism to revise my plans. Although I might have applied legitimately for an author's business allowance, I decided that my own package tours for the book, individually and collectively, spread over two 'holiday years', would obey the rules.

The chief victim of this imposition was my intended ski-tour to Austria, my report on which would have formed one of the book's chapters. As it happens, I have been able to do rather better than that for my readers. I managed to persuade Cherry Burrows, before she set out on a ski holiday to Switzerland, to write a special account of it for my book. The result adorns this chapter. I make no apologies for its length; I have pruned it here and there but, after working over it in detail, I am sure it would be spoiled by further editing.

Cherry, who has helped this book in other ways, is a life-loving brunette; as her story shows, she is an accomplished skier, with a character and sense of humour that seem to thrive on adversity. This is her report.

§ The brochure was bright and attractive, with witty descriptions of low-priced 'chalet' holidays in Switzerland, the essence of which was said to be informality, unfussiness, ability to muck in and, presumably, youth. In search of more details about Verbier and Zermatt, I picked up the telephone. A girl answered and, after much shuffling about, said the particulars were still being typed, and could I ring back a week later? I did so and was put on to another girl, well-informed, well-bred and coolly off-hand. This one deigned to keep me a place in Chalet Mont Blanc in Zermatt for the second fortnight in March, provided that my £5 deposit and completed booking form reached her without delay. The deal clinched, all I had to do was reinforce the seams of my vintage ski pants, collect hopeful stores of sun oil, make feeble attempts at get-fit exercises and swop hair-raising stories with friends of perpendicular, ice-covered ski-runs, including gruesome tales of Zermatt—the Wall of Death, the Galleries and the Black Run.

During this process I changed my job and, my new boss preferring me to take my holiday during the first half of March, I rang the agent to ask if this were possible. No, every chalet in Zermatt was now fully booked—but, as I was putting down the 'phone, a voice shouted, 'Try Mr Henderson of Pimlico.' I was told this man needed another girl in his party and was very nice, so I rang him. The answering gent sounded middle-aged and extremely vague about the whole thing; when I told him my name, he said he would have to give me a pip, haw haw; he asked if I could go and have a medical for insurance purposes and then said he would arrange everything, hee hee. Another member of the party would ring me that evening. It was hard to judge whether the person who rang that night was male or female; my questions got the reply that everything was 'all so very marvellous' and 'all so terribly exciting'. But I gathered the average age of the party was under twenty and, feeling suddenly a bit ancient, I insisted on meeting the ambiguous creature. It promised to ring me the next week to make an appointment. Meanwhile, I had to fork out a three-guinea 'alteration' fee, the agent being determined to pick up every spare guinea from undecided wafflers.

A week passed in silence. I rang the original number, to learn that Mr Henderson was away. His secretary was amazed by my story. Mr Henderson was in his thirties, unmarried and devoid of sexless friends or relations. The average age of his party was in the mid-twenties. The elusive Mr Henderson was evidently not the person to whom I had first spoken. When eventually I reached him, he was politely incredulous about my story and confessed that he had never heard of me, let alone spoken to me; and, although he did need a girl to join his party, he wouldn't dream of asking me to join his group without first meeting me.

There was now a mere fortnight before departure and I was getting desperate. I dressed myself in my slinkiest trouser suit, took tremendous pains with my make-up, polished my flat to an unnatural brilliance and prepared potfuls of steaming coffee while awaiting Mr Henderson. I was not disappointed. He was good-looking, tall, dressed with casual care for the week-end and had that slightly heavy-eyed man-about-town air which is so fetching. Gliding over my polished floors, I fed him with biscuits and bright chatter and hoped I was making the grade. As he got up to go, he smiled and said he was glad he could now stop looking for another girl. He hated asking for it, but could I let him have a further £5 deposit? Of course I could! I was in.

Two more windfalls came my way during this fortnight: I had the opportunity of an extra few days' leave and I came into a small legacy. I arranged to lengthen my holiday. I visited the agent's office; I was told they could *not* accommodate me for any extra days at any of their chalets, nor could they give me a refund if I changed my flight. But my blood was up. I took myself elsewhere and booked on to a scheduled BEA flight; then I looked up the number of a Zermatt hotel and dialled straight through on STD. By luck, they had a cancellation for a single room on the day I wanted, so I wrote to confirm my reservation, packed my bags and laid on extra insurance. I also bought myself an extremely sexy evening trouser-suit.

Tuesday

The journey was a dream and the flight by Trident so
prompt that I had to pocket the sandwich breakfast
I had with me to make way for a rather dried-up lunch,
served at 10.30 in the morning, which we hardly had
time to swallow before landing, ahead of schedule, at
Geneva. An attractive American lady, Betty, also bound
for Zermatt, persuaded me into her first-class compartment on the train from Geneva to Visp; fortified with
apple juice and coffee bought from passing trolleys, we
chatted and gazed out at Lake Geneva as we sped through
the splendidly Victorian lakeside towns of Lausanne,
Vevey and Montreux, all backed by clouds, with the
towering Midi massif rising sheer from the far side, the
pinnacles along its summit lit by occasional shafts of sun.
At the end of the lake we passed steadily along a great
glaciated valley, its steep sides covered with vines on
ancient terraces; at the end of this valley, four hours
out of Geneva, was Visp, under its damp and dripping
cloud, where we waited among the puddles for our train
to Zermatt, watching the sturdy blue-smocked railway
officials at their work, with their clear-eyed and cherubic
faces, as though the cares of the world had passed them
by.

The little train to Zermatt took us up the tortuous
valley, so narrow that we could almost touch the sheer
walls; the cog-wheel clanged into place as we jerked
higher up the mountain, the wooden coaches creaking
round the frequent bends. Now, on one side or the
other, was the turbulent river in which I could see two or
three battered cars, fallen at some time from an invisible
road above; then came the deep snow strewn with the
debris of recent avalanches, fallen rocks, earth, bent and

tumbled trees. It seemed a miracle that none had fallen on the train; as I learned later, this train is stopped at the faintest chance of an avalanche, delaying impatient holiday-makers and interrupting the supplies to anxious hotels.

After a weary, jolting hour, we were in Zermatt. Disappointment: the hotel receptionist declared blandly that no room was reserved for me and, alas, there were no vacancies. Tired, hungry, aware that this extra holiday was costing me a packet, I lost my temper with un-British vehemence—and was promptly allocated a double room for the night. After settling in, I sought supper in the sumptuous Victorian dining-room, adorned with red velvet curtains, sparkling chandeliers, and a crowd of elegantly-dressed visitors. The service was superb and so was the food; I wolfed four courses ravenously, feeling pale and unhealthy among the other radiantly tanned guests. Then to my enormous room, at the end of lofty corridors, a fight with gigantic radiators to reduce the overpowering heat, and into my vast bed with its enveloping duvet, determined to wake refreshed and ready for the next day's exercise.

Wednesday
Surfacing in my ornate room was a great pleasure. I rang for breakfast which appeared within five minutes, borne shoulder-high on a laden tray by a dashing young waiter. There was masses of delicious coffee, cheese, jams, croissants, rolls, rye bread and fresh white butter. Heartened by this spread, I rushed into my ski clothes, struggling with the unfamiliar boot laces; then, into the town to hire skis and buy an *abonnement*.

As I staggered breathlessly under my weighty skis,

making for the Schwarzee cable-car, a voice called me and there was David, a man I had met ski-ing several years before. He hailed a passing taxi—a horse-drawn sleigh, for there are no cars in Zermatt apart from the ambulance; our skis were loaded on the back while we piled in beneath the thick fur rugs. School children jumped on behind for a free ride as we jingled along, but were severely admonished by the driver who lashed his long whip smartly down each side, leaving some rather surprised little boys in a pile on the puddly road.

We crowded into the cable car and swept up the mountain, which looked ominously bare and rocky. With popping ears, I realised that I could hardly remember the first elements of ski-ing. The cold as we came out of the lift was intense and, round the shoulder of the mountain, the wind was fierce and biting. My numbed fingers could barely manage the bindings. Then, with David's help, we set off, my knees knocking and skis all awry. But somehow, without conscious effort, I found myself turning, swinging over the bumps, slipping smoothly down the mountain and, despite driving snow and poor visibility, enjoying the exhilaration of ski-borne flight, the singing hiss through snow, the brittle rattle of ice. They can do it, those poor city-softened limbs, those legs that crawl from bed to tube to office and back again, they can still fly on skis.

We stopped for lunch at a wooden mountain hut, much used by climbers, to devour steaming soup and piled-up plates of frankfurters and sauerkraut at long tables. We found seats near some British RAF ski club enthusiasts and talked of skis, hotels, weather conditions; and I learned how poor the season had been, with rain, avalanches and lack of snow. The world closes in round a ski resort, and there is no call to think of anything beyond the ski-ing and the amusements. I felt very warm and contented.

But pride comes before the fall, and that afternoon I had crash after painful crash in unseen piles of drifted snow. I said good-bye for the present to David and quit the blizzard for the cable car to Zermatt. There I wandered down the picturesque main street, lined with cafés, hotels, shops, both simple and sophisticated, avoiding the streams of horse-drawn sleighs and lethally-carried skis, window-gazing, buying books, chocolate and apple juice. In my hotel, on being asked if I would mind sleeping in the bathroom, my temper flared again, the receptionist giggled nervously, and I was allowed to keep my palatial double room.

I ordered a bath, and enjoyed the ensuing ceremony. A maid ushered me into a cavernous room with a truly enormous bath tub, set on clawed feet, into which I climbed with the help of two steps, swathed in towelling. The maid laid out no less than three enormous thick white towels, plus a selection of face towels. I wallowed in the soft warm water, soaking away the stiffness of unaccustomed exercise, and counted curiously the blue bruises up and down my legs. After a huge and splendid dinner I went thankfully to bed, too exhausted to accept David's invitation to dance.

Thursday
I awoke with a very painful neck and could hardly believe what I saw in the mirror—one side of my face was completely round and hideously sore. In a panic I asked for the doctor by telephone to be told that he was not yet in his surgery; instead, the receptionist sent

up the hotel nurse. She was a comic little woman, almost entirely hidden by an enormous fringe and starched hat, from the bottom of which poked out a long pointed nose, like a dormouse. She threw up her hands in horror at the sight of my face, and in broken English agreed that a doctor must be fetched.

A couple of hours later she returned with a square young man in ski-ing clothes, his face covered with scars, a local equivalent of the London rugger-playing medical student. It seemed obvious to me that I had mumps but he did not agree, telling me to stay in bed five days; he gave me a penicillin injection and a box of pills and said he would come again that evening.

Among my visitors were Betty, my American girl-friend, having a ball, and David, with a revolting spongey swollen leg, the result of a fall in the morning, the story of which kept me occupied for an hour or more. My face became rounder and rounder. As my temperature climbed I changed from one bed to the other. One gentleman, observing my damp state, brought me a clean pair of pyjamas. That evening, and until I left the hotel, the chamber-maid laid the pyjamas on one turned-down bed and my nightie on the other. I had not the heart to disillusion her—she seemed oblivious that most males, seeing my swollen jaw, kept carefully to the far side of the room. The doctor, who had promised to call again, never arrived.

Friday
When I came to, the sun was glowing on the mountain tops. In the afternoon I ventured up but, after one doddery run and a spectacular fall in full view of a crowded restaurant, gave up, and joined Betty with

two garrulous, gum-chewing girl-friends, gee-ing over the steepness of the runs. A bristly-chinned, bespectacled Pennsylvanian philosophy professor plied us with grog and then escorted me back to Zermatt. My fur hood seemed to be hiding my bulging face successfully.

David met me for dinner at the hotel, the Monte Rosa, from which Whymper had set out to climb the Matter-horn, and the base of many other pioneer climbers. Low-ceilinged, with stone flagged floors, in the centre of the main street, this charming hotel has a fine dining-room, long and low, its walls made of panels edged with graceful moulded plaster-work, enclosing mirrors which reflected from every corner the light and sparkle from delicate crystal chandeliers, which in turn reflected the crimson velvet curtains.

Saturday

Up early and to the station to bid my boy-friend farewell. The train was bursting with healthy, home-bound visitors, their luggage and their skis, and the platform was a milling mass of shouting people. David had been kept a seat by two hopeful girl-friends, who seemed momentarily more than put out by my presence. The train got away at last, disappearing down the valley like a centipede with multitudes of waving arms.

I packed, paid my bill (at the rate for a single room), hired a sleigh and set off for the Chalet Grand Lac, a huge forbidding old building, with a bleak hall that smelled of old cooking. The agent's flat was on the first floor and, having left my boots outside the door as a notice demanded, I entered warily. Joanna, a plump, pretty girl was scrubbing the kitchen floor and another, Susan, tall and gloriously blonde, the zip of her jeans undone and her blouse wrongly buttoned, greeted me. The others were not expected until 16.00 hours but they said I could stay, choose my room and unpack. I picked a pleasant two-bed room with a balcony, pine-walled like the rest of the flat. I was given a light lunch and made to feel at home. Afterwards, I sat in a deck chair and soaked in the scorching sun, too tired from my night out to think of ski-ing. Postcards, the chore of any holiday, a wander round the town and back again, to welcome the rest of the party.

Tired and bedraggled, they began by working out the room-sharing problem. The men were three to a room and the girls had the doubles. My room-mate turned out to be Brigid, ash-blonde, a constant smoker and enormously untidy. Our room was immersed, from the first five minutes, in an assortment of her personal belongings which periodically, in exasperation, I pushed under the bed or into cupboards; the room seemed very small indeed from that time on. The party introduced, we sat down at a long, candle-lit table, covered with red-checked plastic, and helped ourselves to a generous meal and large amounts of rough wine.

We seemed an ill-assorted lot and few personalities stood out that evening apart from Jack Henderson, the party leader, looking rather less urbane than I remembered him. His friends of previous ski-parties were an immensely tall and intelligent girl, Angela, from Edinburgh; a publisher, Sam, a fast talker with an amusing drawl; and Jack's flat-mate, Duncan, a solicitor with grey hair, a paunch, pedantic—he was, in fact, only thirty, the kindest fellow imaginable and obviously greatly taken with my room-mate, Brigid. Then, unknown except by acquaintance, was Robert, quiet, boyish, red-haired and boney; Paul, another solicitor, pale, inclined to silence, blinking behind huge spectacles; and last, the baby of the party, Diana, a nervous, tiny bird-like girl who was to change beyond recognition after a few days and become our star dancer. We drank a great deal more wine and chattered away, presided over by our two chalet girls, who answered our endless questions with patience and good humour. An enjoyable first evening.

Sunday

Having sorted ourselves out over coffee, rolls and cherry jam, we set forth in clusters of what we guessed to be similar grades of skiers. The weather was overcast, with occasional sunshine, unnaturally warm, and we bashed up and down the Gornergrat runs, my few days' ski-ing taking me effortlessly ahead of the others. Lunch in the sun at the crowded, jostling Riffelberg café, a first taste of our invariable midday meals of heavy bread sandwiches and boiled eggs, washed down with delicious Ovomaltine. Why does Ovaltine in England bear no resemblance to the creamy continental brew?

At tea-time, after more ski-ing, we indulged in *glüh-wein*, that famous steaming, sweet, alcoholic drink, and staggered our way homeward. And what an anti-climax it was; after the excitement of the notorious Galleries—that long narrow track alongside the railway, on the side of a precipice, along which it is fatally easy to gather tremendous speed, hoping fervently not to find the way blocked by fallen bodies—the snow took on the consistency of wet sugar, in which our tired legs could hardly turn. In places, it gave out altogether, so that we were climbing over tree roots, scraping over rocks and falling in muddy heaps on the turns. These conditions remained on the lower slopes throughout our stay, except that the slush turned later to ice.

Home at last, I collapsed exhausted on my bed. I was woken by another visitor, Mark, just arrived in Zermatt, an acquaintance from the previous year's holiday. I felt too tired to go out with him but, after dinner in the chalet with quantities of wine, I felt revived enough to go with Jack to visit a mountaineering friend at the Monte Rosa for coffee and brandy. Then, towards midnight, on to the Kanne, a dark place with a noisy Germanic band and seething dance floor, where we met the other members of our chalet party. And so, rather late, to bed.

Monday

As usual, the family in the flat above began their war-dance in ski-boots at 07.00 hours and then, in case any of us still slept, moved all their furniture from A to B and back again. It was a warm and cloudy day and I plodded with Robert, Jack, Sam and Angela up to the Schwarzee lift station. We bumbled up and down the long easy runs beneath the Matterhorn, and thence to a small mountain-climbers' hut for lunch. These huts, slightly off the beaten track, serve the most excellent food at a low price to those who know of them. An entire German family opposite us, from grandfather to grand-children, downed their food and beer with great relish, peering glumly at our miserable sandwiches. The old man, seeing me nod in the warm atmosphere, leaned over the table and said '*Müde*—Tired?' I was, and I returned to the town and slept under my duvet in peace, until the tea-party guests arrived.

Tuesday and Wednesday

One look at the drizzling rain, and I stayed in bed, not feeling my brightest. As the day wore on, my temperature soared and a doctor was called. He turned out to be a plump old gentleman, apparently stuffed with fifty years' accumulation of sauerkraut and sausages, his eyebrows like bushy radar aerials and a prolific growth of whiskers in his ears. But he looked me over sympathetically, produced some pills and told me I could get up again tomorrow. No diagnosis. Bill, 25 francs.

The next day was much the same, though the weather became colder and brighter; I felt disinclined to get out of bed in the morning but joined the tea-party, wrapped bulbously in my duvet, and held court from the only armchair. Mark produced bottles of vitamin C tablets and promised me dinner when I was better.

Thursday

I woke up, recovered but wobbly, fit enough to potter around. Duncan had given up ski-ing to pursue photography, with a host of complicated equipment which he explained to me at length. We set off in the wet driving wind to photograph trains, his other passion. I wandered back along the river, behind the bright new Zermatt hotels, past a jumbled mass of old wooden houses and cow sheds. After tea, I set off for a party at Chalet Bellevue, a rival agent's establishment, run on lines similar to our own. The entrance, through dirty manure-heaped yards, was bleak and unlit. Upstairs, we paid two francs and our toothmugs were filled with *glüh-wein*. In two small rooms there was a smokey English crowd, jammed tightly together, the noise so great it was hard to be coherent. I was about to leave in disgust when I ran into a fabulous giant-like fellow, but as he seemed to be attached to another girl, I came home with Jack who, half tight, kept falling in the slush. We had a dinner of garlicky steak and bananas during which Jack did his best to tempt me to go to the Village. I declined. On my way to bed, an odd bespectacled man, announcing himself as Theophilus, wandered in with a whisky bottle and ensconced himself on my bed. After a while, I persuaded him to leave, and he found better luck in the next room where Joanna and Duncan entertained him until the small hours.

Friday
The faithful Angela got us up. Sodden day; umbrellas in the streets. Brigid and I decided to ski up the Gornergrat railway, despite the weather; I felt I must not miss any more precious sport. Driving snow and blizzard at the top station and crowds of people. Heavy snow on the runs and no visibility. Wall of Death littered with fallen people. I caught a glimpse of Brigid plunging head-first down the Wall, clasped in the arms of a stranger. He turned out to be Bill, an American psychology student, a brilliant skier and afterwards a regular tea visitor.

Lunch at Riffelberg with Betty and other dripping Americans and then, seeing the gorgeous giant from the Chalet Bellevue party and learning that he was in Brigid's class, I decided to join it too. The ski-instructor was a little man with a checked hat who led us slowly and comfortably down the lovely Findeln run, known as the gun barrel because of its narrow steepness. Instead of straining one's eyes into the blizzard, one had only to follow blindly in the wake of the instructor. The gorgeous giant accepted our invitation to tea and asked us

99

to meet his friends but, having committed myself to dinner with Mark, I had sadly to refuse.

Clad in my new trouser suit, I set out for Mark's hotel, a luxurious new building on the river. A runaway horse, its harness dangling, galloped past me across the bridge and I wondered where were the sleigh and its astonished occupants. Mark, and a friend, Tim, entertained me to a fine dinner in the candlelit grill-room, the meat roasted on a spit over an open fire, with an abundance of delectable local wine. Then, merrily, home.

Saturday

I hurried off to meet Mark, his friend Tim, and their guide, Oscar, a vast elderly man with a filthy white cap and a cigar. We set off towards Schwarzee and saw the Matterhorn glowing and sunlit behind a thin wraith of cloud. The cables, glinting in the sun, reached up and were lost in cloud; they looked like a lift to heaven. But there was a fierce wind on Trocknersteg and it was very cold. Oscar set forth, turning like a tank, and we trundled along behind him. Alas, Tim was a beginner and we spent icy minutes on every corner waiting for him. The snow had drifted deeply down the runs but there were occasional sheets of wind-blown ice, and expert skiers and beginners alike were tumbling around the mountain in the treacherous conditions.

After lunch at Schwarzee, Donald, the mountaineer, joined us and Oscar, aglow with Mark's wine, made weighty compliments to the colour of my eyes, confiding that he had climbed the Matterhorn over two hundred times. I opted to ski with Donald, who led me off the piste across the wastes of blown snow into the cloud and gloom. After ten plodding minutes he confessed that he had left his compass behind. But he was as sure as a goat and, having recognised a rocky outcrop, we flew down virgin snow, our skis buried beneath it, making huge wide turns, until we could see the ant-covered piste below us. My trouser zip and its hook decided to part company at that point, but Donald rose to the occasion and, reaching into his enormous haversack, found a narrow piece of climbing rope. This I wound many times round my waist and, as long as I remained standing it saved the day. Whenever I fell, however, the whole process had to be repeated.

Sunday

The whole crowd of us set off together, in good weather, to find depressingly long queues at the lift. Abnormal queues were to be our fate from now on; poor snow throughout the Alps was forcing people up to the higher resorts, and after so much bad weather any hint of sun would bring every man-jack of us out.

At the top station we took the new Furgjoch drag lift up the glacier to the top of the Theodulpass, on the border of Italy. The view there is breath-taking; perched high on the top of the pass, I looked across the shallow bowl of Cervenia, swarming with skiers, to the Alpine peaks, grey, white and blue, stretching to infinity. On the left, the Breithorn, covered by caps of shining green ice; then the massive Monta Rosa, highest mountain in the valley. To the right, the Matterhorn from an unfamiliar angle, its east ridge towering darkly above us, the challenge (and death) of many climbers. Behind, the panorama of Zermatt, its valley stretching away to the horizon.

We played on the glacier all morning, performing well

on the wide slopes, the experts taking it straight, at high speed. Then, the wind began to rise and the cold became intense.

Later, at tea, we found Angela, badly frost-bitten, her face puffy, purple and oozing liquid. A stranger, seeing the first signs, had quickly rubbed her face in snow. She was confined indoors for several days, attended by a doctor practised in mountain ailments. Sam, dancing with excitement, had met an ex girl-friend, Sophia, from a previous ski-ing party, and was entertaining her. She was tiny, with a mass of black hair, and gazed at Sam with great solemnity, while politely eating our crumbly slices of bread and treacle. Although she had a boy-friend in attendance, Sam was unashamedly entranced.

This was our night for eating out, a condition of the holiday enabling our chalet girls to take an evening off. We set off for Zermatterhof, Zermatt's plushiest hotel, where Duncan had booked a table. Like children out of school, in our modest Sunday best, we trooped into the elegant dining-room, trying not to be intimidated by all the jewels and evening gowns. The menu muddled us and the men had arguments about the wine, but the head waiter humoured us and we were soon tucking into delectable consommé, salmon with 'angel sauce', steak and an elaborate dessert, with second and third helpings, served willingly by no less than four underlings. Luxury! Over coffee on the dance-floor, we joined the sugar daddies and their popsies, cavorting around the glass pillars. But Auntie Duncan remained seated, surrounded by scruffy piles of notes and coins, as he counted painstakingly, with knitted brows, waving at us from time to time to come and contribute our due share.

Monday

A ski-school day with Sam, the two of us assigned to the care of tiny, brown, bird-like Anne-Marie, mother of grown sons. In the Gornergrat train, a cosy cocoon in the howling wind and lashing snow, we sat beside a bullet-headed young man from the chalet Bellevue, who seemed unconcerned by the fact that only one bath served all ten of them and that he smelled like it. Out in the blizzard, bending to struggle with my frozen bindings, the zip on my last-remaining trousers gave up the ghost. No one had a pin or any spare rope. I thanked heaven for my woollen long johns of the same colour and prayed my trousers would remain more or less in place. The conditions were extreme; without goggles, my eyes streamed and the tears froze on my cheeks. Off the summit it was easier and Anne-Marie, inspecting us closely for frost-bite, exercised us in parallel turns. Mercilessly she shouted 'Jump, jump,' and, to me, furiously, my pants wrinkling baggily at the knees, '*Why* do you not make more movement?'

Our relief on reaching the Riffelberg café was enormous. *Glüh-wein* and grog soon thawed the icicles from our faces. In the town, I began the serious search for ski-pants, discovering in the sophisticated, scented shops an array of the world's most desirable ski-clothes, beautifully cut trousers, bewitching figure-hugging anoraks and sumptuous fur accessories. With Paul's appreciative help, it was no trouble to find several trousers to suit me—I chose the tightest—but it was galling to lack the cash to replace the rest of my hard-worked apparel. Here was the ideal place to fit oneself out for ski-ing, with prices lower and style and quality higher than anywhere in London.

From the shops to the Monte Rosa, to the private party of a charming Englishman, Kim, about 6 feet 7 inches tall, a pleasant change from our usual free-for-all scrums. Kim's friends were cosmopolitan and cultured; I was introduced to new people, among them the wife of the superintendent of the lifts and rescue teams in Zermatt, who told us fascinating stories of life and death; Albrecht, an attractive German lawyer with flawless English and a sparkling humour; and Stefan, a swarthy Italian interpreter, student of politics, son of his country's ambassador to Peru, who attached himself limpet-like to my elbow.

But Paul and Sam whisked me away to The Village, noisy and overcrowded, where I timed my dances with each so as not to offend the other. Then to Elsie's place, meeting-point of all Zermatt, small, intimate, personal, presided over by Elsie who produced vast dishes of aromatic snails and goblets of wine for our bedtime snack. All three of us, weaving home with linked arms, fell in a heap on the fresh snow.

Tuesday

With my new pants and a splitting head, I rejoined Anne-Marie's class, grown in the sunshine to fourteen strong, a cross-section of people and nationalities, including a minute Japanese gentleman, bedecked from top to toe with shiny new equipment—cap, goggles, knapsack, clip boots, racing skis—who spoke meticulous upper-class English. Poor chap, as we set off across the flat snow, he promptly fell face-first all in a heap. Having picked him up, dusted his glasses, replaced his cap and fixed his skis, the rest of us sped off behind Anne-Marie, along a steep but easy traverse, to the sheltered Hornli run, there to practise our stops and turns. After twenty minutes, a tiny figure appeared round the corner of the mountain stepping gingerly down the traverse. Unwilling to admit that he hardly knew how to ski, he made the excuse that his new boots were hurting him.

We returned to our exercises, to be interrupted after a while by a shout and the sight of Anne-Marie rushing in pursuit of the Japanese gentleman, his skis wide apart, his arms waving, sliding backwards towards a precipice. Rescued, he tried bravely to persuade us that he was, in fact, a champion skier, a little out of practice, who had not quite got the hang of his new skis. Minutes later. looking round for him, he was nowhere to be seen. We hoped he had not committed hari-kari on his ski-sticks or fallen down a crevasse; a couple of thousand years hence, perhaps, the local inhabitants will be surprised to find at the mouth of the glacier an exquisitely-equipped Japanese, a little man who strayed into class five instead of class one.

At lunch I sat with a lean Shropshire dentist, making do with a bowl of soup and dry bread as, hungrily, he watched me pick at my sandwiches. Unlucky victim of the £50 travel allowance, he found he could spend no more than two francs on his meal; he eagerly accepted my discarded boiled egg, mashed into an unrecognisable mess by my constant falls, and this he wolfed, shell and all, following it down with my spare chocolate. He was injured that afternoon by a broken lift bar, which cut his face, while we were waiting for a tow, and I did not see him again. Anne-Marie sorted out our ungainly group, demoting all but three, of which I was proud to be one.

In the evening, tired of the banter and lack of comfort

in our chalet, I called on Mark and was welcomed by a hug and drinks, and an enormous dinner of salmon and *chateaubriand* steak. Plans for an early night fell through when I found the American, Bill, reclining on my bed, deep in conversation with Brigid. Paul joined us and we sat up much too late, talking, over a bottle of whisky.

Wednesday

Sam, excited by the prospect of Sophia and the hope of sunshine, woke us at 06.30 hours for our expedition into Italy, and twelve of us made early tracks for the lift. We were not a minute too soon, for by 08.00 hours the queues stretched, eight deep, far down the road. From the top of the glacier-lift we made off down and around the famous Theodulpass, used from the Stone Age as a trading route and well known to the Romans; then we plodded up the glacier, sweating in the heat, to the Italian lift. Here we were obviously on foreign snow— brilliantly clad girls and their fancy men bombed along in atrocious style, shouting and waving their sticks.

We sped down the long slopes, keeping a wary eye open for the whizz-kids, a dangerous Italian speciality, until we reached the village of Cervinia, a cluster of modern pine-built flats and chalets of outstanding comfort and design. Tired and hungry, we trailed through the streets, unable to agree where to settle down to our pasta and chianti.

We found a smart restaurant and sat ourselves down to mountains of spaghetti and a few swallows of chianti, and staggered back to our skis. On the way, we saw an elderly couple on their balcony, the man dressed in emerald green with white stripes and the lady in orange stripes, both wearing cowboy hats, taking elaborately posed photographs of one another. Irked by our mocking faces, the old man picked up an outsize orange from his laden lunch-table and threw it at us, but it landed on a snow-covered roof. Sam, not to be beaten, clambering on to Paul's hands, reached the orange but fell off the roof into a deep fall of snow. The orange stayed in my pocket until the summit of the pass, where it tumbled down the precipice, gathering snow all the way.

The queues for the Italian lifts were endless, made worse by the hordes of young men who had come from afar to practise for an international ski race. They played every possible trick to jump the queues and several fights broke out with objectors. They were a rough crowd, flamboyant in skin-tight elasticised cat suits, often of satin and always in garish colours, with crash helmets imitated by every Italian child. After long hours on our feet, we reached the top. It was bitterly cold as we raced down, to find another lengthy queue waiting for the cable car towards Zermatt. Further delays at each interchange station in the freezing evening, with wet boots and no shelter; it was miserable. Five hours of a gorgeous day had been spent queueing or in lifts, against which we had clocked up little more than one hour's ski-ing; and the outing, costing us each about thirty francs, had not been cheap. Mark turned up for tea with a bottle of whisky; the rest of the group went to a Ski Club of Great Britain party, while I took the opportunity of enjoying a bath—a rare luxury.

Thursday

I hurried off to join my class at the lift and queued alongside a tall American psychiatrist who invited me to accompany him to Cervinia. Determined to improve my ski-ing, I stuck to Addy, my blue-eyed young instructor. The rest of the class was gathered at the top; a Swiss girl, two muscular Germans and a small insignificant Briton, the dunce of the class. Addy led us off at a hair-raising speed to the steepest run in Zermatt, the Black run, famous for its avalanches. We sped down, Addy shouting and admonishing. 'My dear girl, why are your skis not together?' 'Bend, jump.' 'You are not *working*.' Sweat poured down my face and my legs trembled with fatigue. I felt shamed by the two splendid Germans who skied faultlessly. The tallest, Kurt, took upon himself the role of my protector; time and again, he picked me up after plunging falls down the sheer icy gully.

We lunched at the Aroleid restaurant, reached only by one of three precipitous runs and, consequently, uncrowded. Kurt and Addy and I lounged on deck-chairs, watching Dalmatian puppies tumbling in the sun and a shepherd, cradling an early lamb, driving his sheep down to the lower, uncovered, pastures. Addy was persuaded to talk about his summer occupation as a mountain guide, and of his family, one of the oldest in Zermatt. He and all the other Zermatters I encountered were charming people, unassuming, capable and typical of true mountaineers. Then we set off again, first down the Aroleid run, so steep that the surface seethed with the moving snow which each skier dislodged; finally, down the Black run once again; and thence, thankfully, home—exhausted, bruised, but all of a piece.

After changing, Paul and I collected Mark and we joined an exclusive party organised by Jack and Sam for Sophia and her boy-friend. Sam danced, bewitched, with his Sophia, undeterred by the blond boy-friend, now revealed as her fiancé. The exclusiveness of the party was spoiled by the unintended arrival of the remainder of the group, so Mark and I detached ourselves from all the sixth-form intrigue and sat together over coffee in a small bar, wondering at the way the English choose to enjoy themselves.

Friday

Our last day in Zermatt was sunny and, miraculously, there were no queues. I abandoned my class to ski with Jack and Sam on the Theodul glacier, flowing blue beneath the east face of the Matterhorn. The cold was severe. Alone on this long unpisted run, Jack led us between the gaping crevasses over the crusted snow, wind-blown into ripples so that our skis juddered over the bumpy surface. We gazed at the lowering loose face of the Matterhorn and at the Hornlihütte, perched on the approaching ridge, and wondered at the thought that three climbers were at that moment creeping up the hidden north face, their third day out, in day-time temperatures far below freezing. The glaciers hung blue-green and menacing above us as we fled away from them, on to the crowded homely piste.

The cold was so intense that I spent the afternoon thankfully returning my skis and packing my clothes. For tea, with Mark I had *raclettes*, a traditional Valais speciality of melted cheese eaten with baked potatoes, small onions and gherkins. Washed down with wine, it is a good dish but, like haggis, it needs cold and exercise to make the gluey stuff palatable. Then, for a farewell drink with Sam, Paul and Sophia at the Stockhorn café and back to our own party, a grim whisky-in-a-tooth-mug affair. The men became tight as the evening wore on and my ideas of early abed were sunk by their pawing attentions. Brigid slept while the boys fooled in our room but sleep for me came late.

Saturday

Woken cruelly by Joanna at 05.00 hours, we piled our luggage on the waiting sleighs and followed them in the dawn down the quiet streets, the snow high, soft and falling thickly. It was like a Russian scene, the black-hooded sleigh with its long-coated driver, his head sunk into a deep collar and the emerging people, fur-hatted and booted, scurrying about their business. The train filled with holiday-makers and, having waved good-bye to our chalet girls, we dozed our way to Visp and then relaxed in the more comfortable coaches of the main line train.

The airport seethed with tourists. Our bunch, hollow-eyed and scruffy, sat around a soggy pile of sandwiches, drinking wine and snapping each other until weigh-in time. The flight home was uneventful, apart from a jolly man who sat next to me and made endless jokes, and a great address-swopping session. It was with relief that we arrived, exhausted, in England, away from the bitter cold, to be welcomed by spring flowers and mild sunshine.

The 'chalet' fortnight had been eventful enough but, due partly to bad luck—my illness and poor weather—I cannot count it among my best holidays. It had its good moments and, certainly, was inexpensive. The 'package' price for the two weeks, including all fares, full board, wine, lodging and an *abonnement* for all the ski lifts, was

£72 9s 6d and the hire of wooden skis came to £3 3s. It was a good buy—the *abonnement* alone, bought locally, would have cost about £20. A girl needs pocket money to the tune of about £15—a man rather more—for extra drinks and meals, evenings out and personal shopping. So, the all-in bill adds up more or less to £100. Informality was the rule, not so easily found in the larger Swiss hotels, and we made the most of the free drinks and tea parties. There was constant companionship, an important asset for a lone visitor in a large resort, and I made firm friends.

The inherent disadvantages, however, were numerous. Gravest was the lack of domestic amenities: no hot water in the bedroom and only limited supplies in the two bathrooms; no lavatories or lighted mirrors except in the bathrooms, causing urgent queues—and, once inside, embarrassed haste, knowing that others were waiting at the door. In the bedrooms, which otherwise were adequate, the space for clothes and accessories was too small, and the rooms were not kept clean.

But the worst defect was insufficient heating; our wet ski clothes were never dry and our boots remained damp from one end of the holiday to the other—purgatory on the cold mornings. Susan and Joanna took pride in their cooking and gave us quantities of fresh vegetables, but we could have done without the over-rich, over-sweet chocolate puddings; most nights I had to secrete mine away in a paper bag. And the stodgy packed sandwich lunches—even after strenuous exercise they were hard to stomach.

The other problems were questions of temperament. It was impossible to relax in peace or privacy, to go early and undisturbed to bed or to lie in late in the morning—

and, contrary to popular belief, an energetic skier
needs more sleep than usual, not less. One was expected
to stick with the group most of the time or be thought a
spoil-sport. For a determined skier this was a handicap;
one wasted precious hours waiting around for the others.
As a boisterous young all-British party, we tended to
attract and team up socially with compatriots of the
same ilk, cutting ourselves off from the cosmopolitan life
around us; we were abroad, but hardly touched by
foreign influence.

And gang chemistry, in a chalet setting, seems to bring
out the overgrown schoolboy lurking just below the
surface of the English character; our flickering lights of
maturity were too well hidden under bushels of juvenile
bantering and adolescent larking about. One can work
too hard at having fun; it was, perhaps, significant that
the member of our group who seemed to enjoy it all the
most was the youngest.

But I do not regret it, and am grateful to Jack for
admitting me to his party. He was an able and convivial
leader. Surviving all the hazards, he remains a carefree
bachelor and, I hope, the decoy for fresh coveys of
twittering birds in the years ahead.

Chapter Seven
Tulip Time

WE were a few minutes late to supper that first evening in Holland. By the time my son, Rupert, aged eleven, and I reached the hotel dining room, the other members of the party, thirty-five in all, were well spooned into their soup. We were shown to a table laid for five. Already seated were a young fair-haired South African girl, travelling alone, and a greying elderly couple from Yorkshire. Everyone was hungry and, until stomachs were satisfied, there was little tendency to talk. The veal was excellent, the service swift and friendly. Then, over the ice-cream, a ripple of chatter spread across the room.

At our table, the girl told us shyly that this was her first trip to the Continent. She had been in London, studying sociology, for three months and, after a year, would return to her own country. Her remarks encouraged the old couple to admit that they, too, were venturing into Europe for the first time. These two had never before been out of England; besides breaking foreign ground, they had that morning flown in their first aeroplane. Some day!

This sturdy pair, well into their sixties, had risen at 05.00 hours and walked, with their suitcases, over two miles to the railway station. 'The neighbours offered us a lift but it seemed a shame to get them up so early,' said the lady amiably. In London, for them, another walk to the coach station near King's Cross, starting point of our tour; the coach ride to Southend; the short hop by Viscount to Rotterdam; a full afternoon of sightseeing by coach in Holland; a quick wash at the Utrecht hotel; and supper. It was now nearly 21.00 hours; if they were tired or excited or homesick, they were not showing it. 'It's been a lovely day and we did so enjoy the flight,' beamed the lady. Her husband looked at his watch and stood up. 'Well, come on love,' he urged. 'Time for a look round the town.'

On the face of it, one coach tour might seem much like any other, but, as I was discovering, this one was different in several respects to the tour which I described in my first chapter. We had crossed the Channel by air, not by sea; we were taking a look at only one country, instead of four; we were to be based at the one hotel throughout the trip. The tour's duration was a mere four days, and was relatively cheap; and it was designed to attract the first-timer or the less adventurous foreign-going tripper. It was taking place in a concentrated form, at a peak of the local tourist season and, accordingly, had

114

a more sausage-machine quality than the previous tour. While it lasted, it was to prove just as arduous, if not more so, but, despite a tight schedule, it was less deftly organised.

Our courier this time was a young Dutch undergraduate on vacation, well briefed for the job but by no means a professional; he was amusing and attentive, his commentary was witty and intelligent, but he failed to assert himself as our leader. In consequence, we tended to be unpunctual and to delay the programme, the victim in any case of unexpected traffic jams on the overcrowded roads. There was virtually no provision for coffee and tea breaks and, in marked contrast with the earlier trip, no allowance was made for several hours on end for those needing a lavatory; and there was hardly time before the evening meal, after a long day out, for a wash and none at all for a change of clothes.

But we gained in the sense that a remarkably busy programme was crammed into the three days on Dutch soil. We fitted in conducted tours of a Delft pottery, a clog factory, a bulb farm, a flower auction, a cheese farm, a diamond factory, the model village of Madurodam, the Amsterdam canals and the famous Keukenhof tulip park. We had time also to wander around the fishing village of Volendam, the farming hamlet of Broek in Waterland and the Rijksmuseum; to go shopping in Rotterdam; and to see something of Utrecht in the evenings. All this, at a basic all-in cost of £20 a head.

Our trip was blessed, and cursed, by glorious weather. So much trooping about would have been a gloomy ordeal in the rain. The nuisance was that, coinciding with a local public holiday week-end and with the moment when most of the tulips were fully in bloom, the sun brought out the car-borne crowds in their thousands from cities near and far, German and Belgian as well as Dutch. Our own agent was adding cheerfully to the congestion by running simultaneously a dozen or more air-coach tours direct from centres all over England. The Dutch are patient and methodical but the long traffic blocks, the queues at the entrance gates and the shuffling masses within were almost too much for them and, for us, took some of the shine off the outing.

Even so, there were few grumbles and the consensus of opinion in our coach had it that it was all a jolly good show. Our group, mainly in the forty-five to sixty-five age range, consisted largely of unmarried women, travelling in pairs. There were four married couples of the same vintage, one of them accompanied by a mentally retarded grown-up son. There was one young married couple, with a docile five-year-old boy in tow. All these were from the east and south-east of England. The only foreigners, apart from the pretty South African girl at our hotel table, were a diligently fact-seeking American married couple in their early thirties.

The tour was too short for the group to achieve much cohesion but it was a merry and relaxed party from the outset. We were ordinary folk out for simple fun, keen to praise rather than to criticise, and all mercies, however small, were thankfully received. There was much good-natured banter and badinage, and the slightest witticism, whether by members of the group or by our escorts, was greeted with eager laughter. We were tireless in pursuit of the somewhat onerous programme, lapping up every experience befalling us and, although good manners were observed at all times, comments on the passing scene were made with hearty gusto.

'Oh, look! Isn't it lovely?' cried one of the women in the seat behind, as we drove through the residential outskirts of The Hague. 'All those nice houses and their gardens and the blossom—it really is, it's just like Bournemouth.'

'Well, it was a bit of a fight,' remarked an old spinster when we reassembled after surviving the Keukenhof crush. 'The worst part was the toilets,' agreed her friend. 'I mean—to have to wait an hour in a queue for a quick drip, that's really terrible, isn't it?'

On the way back from Amsterdam to Utrecht, as we passed through a lush rural area, our courier told us about the rich merchants' country houses on their well-tended land beside the canal. A red-faced lady, with a voice like sandpaper, who had readily acquired a taste for *Oude Jenever*, nudged her friend and confided loudly, 'Well, I must say; what with Rembrandt and all these posh houses, we do seem to have come up in the world, don't we?'

As we approached the airport on the last morning, summing up was in full swing. Four of the old girls had evidently done Utrecht proud the previous night. 'Oh, yes, I do like a bit of night life now and then,' cackled one of them. 'That cabaret was very nice but,' lowering her voice, 'wasn't it a shame that only the girls came on in the nude.' 'Even so,' came the reply, 'it was a sight more fun than a wet evening in the Scillies, I dare say.'

But the prize goes to two old dears explaining quietly to one another why they had chosen this particular tour. 'I wanted to come mid-week, when it would have been less crowded,' said one, 'but they told me there's a shortage of husbands on week-days—there's usually more to go round at the week-end when the men aren't working.' There was a pause while they glanced coldly around the coach. 'But, really it couldn't have been worse. Hardly a husband between the lot of us on this trip—and a crumby bunch they are, at that.'

The other complaints were less heart-rending. One skinny grandmother said plaintively, several times, that she would feel happier if the driver would stop talking to the courier and keep his eye on the road. Several members, unaccustomed to foreign drinking habits and to the few opportunities for refreshment, were suffering from lack of tea. Our visit to the Rijksmuseum was heaven-sent; most of us, after a quick nip around the picture galleries, made a bee-line for the restaurant. When Rupert and I got there, we joined the old pair from Yorkshire, ecstatically devouring rich cream cakes, the table littered with tea pots, water jugs and all the accoutrements of mid-afternoon happiness. They admitted without a flicker of shame that the art galleries could go hang; the chance to get outside a few cuppas was attraction enough.

For me, the chief irritation was an error made by the agent with my room reservations. I had applied for, and been assured that I would be given, a twin-bedded double room with private shower and WC but, on the first evening in Utrecht, Rupert and I were checked into a room with a double bed and no lavatory. The receptionist received my protest with ill grace but, after much persuasion, transferred us to better accommodation.

The extent and variety of the sight-seeing programme and the long mileage covered in following it allowed us, in the three days or so, to glimpse many facets of Holland and of the Dutch way of life. The trip by boat around the Amsterdam canals is a revelation. I had done it before but still found it full of pleasant surprises, reminding me of that city's Venetian quality, its fine architecture, the tranquillity of its backwaters and the dynamism of its character. Amsterdam, one of the world's attractive cities, is rich with features and amenities to suit every taste. And, considering its proximity and the friendly attitude of its inhabitants to England, it is an ideal destination for Britons who want to go abroad inexpensively, without getting too far out of their depth.

The Dutch have a genius for creating the necessities of life in a small congested country without offending the eye. Drab industrial areas and gloomy suburbs hardly exist. The houses and flats, with their wide uncurtained picture windows, decorated with shrubs and potted plants, invite the sunshine to come in and the passer-by to feel welcome, giving the lie to the idea that the Dutch are a dour and secretive race. They are a genial and lively people and, although out to exploit tourism to the ultimate, they have a genuinely charming and good-humoured touch with the visitor.

Volendam was the only exception to this rule. This fishing village is a touristic horror, with its inhabitants arrayed in national costume, its souvenir shops, its tatty bars and its streets choked with cars and coaches. And, behind the façade of tinsel and tawdriness, there lies a village of no great distinction. The factories and farms that we visited, taking our turn with other queueing coach-loads, were interesting and the guides who took us round them showed none of the boredom which they must have felt in coping daily with streams of vaguely curious visitors. We were duly impressed by the well-rehearsed clap-trap, including Broek in Waterland's claim to be the cleanest dairy village in Europe, where even the cows were said to receive a daily bath.

The best bit of fun for Rupert, apart from a view of the shipping in the port of Amsterdam, was Madurodam, a generous slice of Dutch life in miniature. On view are working scale models of Dutch airports, railways, highways, factories and city neighbourhoods; it is imaginatively laid out in the open air, in a pleasant sheltered enclosure.

My son did not, however, wholly share my enthusiasm for the flower auction. Here, in a huge covered building, cut flowers arrive in the evening from suppliers throughout the district and, during the night, are sorted and labelled, ready for the auctions which start before dawn. In the auction rooms, the buyers sit at tiers of desks from which they can see the produce as it is brought forward in quick succession on trolleys. The 'bidding' starts high, instead of low, the proposed price being shown on a giant automatic clock-face; as the clock's hand descends down the price range, the first buyer who stops it, by means of a press-button under his desk, wins that particular item of produce. His identity, the reference number of the item and the purchase price, are recorded mechanically on a card and, by the time the buyer leaves the auction room, his goods are ready, packaged and invoiced, in the despatch department. By noon, the flowers are on their way to the buyers' customers; those for export, which number billions a year, are sent by road direct to Schipol airport, to be on sale in the flower shops of Western Europe and North America that same afternoon.

The advertised highlight of our tour was the visit to

the Keukenhof park. The brochure had told us that we would be free to wander 'through sixty acres of colour and beauty and see more than a million tulips of over a thousand varieties'. After a walk we could 'sit out in the Park Restaurant amidst all the colour and joy of spring'. Unfortunately, the dominant colours on the Sunday of our visit were those of the sunburned faces and of the staid clothes worn by the thousands of milling tourists; of the famous tulips we saw little. The crowd shuffling eight deep along the pathways was carried aimlessly along by its own momentum, and as for sitting in the restaurant, there was no hope of that. It would be nice to return some day to enjoy the flowers.

I was reminded of a remark made by our agent's cheerful girl representative, who checked us into the coach at King's Cross on the first day. Teasingly, she said she couldn't imagine why we wanted to travel all the way to Holland to see some tulips. There was a fine display near Southend, she told us. Why go further? We all laughed at her little joke but it needed the Keukenhof experience to bring it home.

Chapter Eight
On the Ocean Wave

16.00 The long steam-hauled boat train pulled out of Waterloo and set a south-westerly course for Southampton, speed 55 knots. My coach was clean and warm but there was no water in the lavatory. A dingy help-yourself buffet car distributed weak tea in plastic mugs to queueing passengers. An old lady in my compartment said she had been waiting more than two hours at Waterloo, having thought that 16.00 hours meant two o'clock. Later, she asked if Las Palmas was an island and whether we should be landing there in small boats. The genial clerk from the shipping line, who came to check the tickets, warned that they were rather fierce about currency smuggling at Southampton. 'If they pick on you, your wallet may be searched—and if there's no loot there, you may be searched all over.'

17.45 As it happened they didn't—and I wasn't. An hour and three-quarters out of Waterloo the train crept quietly through the docks into the giant ship's shadow. I will call her the *Old Lady*. In the summer she has been doing what she was built to do—steaming to and fro along a well-known route as a passenger liner. Off-season when not re-fitting, her lot has been cruises. In her heyday, when only madmen flew, she played hostess to the great figures of the world—millionaires, ministers, duchesses and film stars. Her vast ornate public rooms were designed to provide a splendid setting for splendid people.

The mark of most of us today, a motley cruise-bound lot, was hardly splendour. The formalities at Southampton however, gave a fillip to our self esteem. The customs hall was luxurious and we were shepherded gently, in a slow-moving throng, through the barriers, to be smiled at briefly by benign officials. Then, over the covered gangway into the ship's foyer, where cheerful stewards dispersed us to our quarters. Fourteen minutes after leaving the train I was in my stateroom, and a few minutes later my baggage joined me. I had not been troubled with my baggage since the porter took it in hand when I left my taxi at Waterloo. Flawless organisation, promising hospitality—an encouraging start.

18.30 The ship's bells summoned us to lifeboat stations. An officer spoke to us on the captain's behalf, warning us kindly but firmly of the ocean's perils. Cigarettes thrown overboard might enter an open porthole and burn a bunk—or ignite its occupant;

children climbing on the rail would end their days in Davy Jones's locker; in emergency we had only to collect our life jackets and report promptly but calmly at our proper station, and all would be well. The best of British reassurance to you all! My daughter, Caroline, aged thirteen, afloat for the first time ever, was duly impressed—and not least by the gorgeous flowers 'with the compliments of the staff' which awaited her return below decks. She had a cabin adjoining mine; the stewardess showed her the bells, the light switches and all the busy gadgets. If in need, she had only to ring.

Our accommodation was modest enough, inside staterooms near the ship's bowels, though mine boasted a cosy private bathroom. The fares for this cruise ranged from £500 in a main deck suite to £70 in a D deck cubby-hole; Caroline and I, well down the scale, were paying £108 and £128 respectively. In common with all the passengers, we enjoyed the run of the entire vessel— two lounges, four bars, two restaurants, library, drawing room, writing room, cinema, two swim pools, gymnasium, four shops, a playroom, kennels and acres of deck space. On every hand a steward to guide, serve or beam a friendly smile. The *Old Lady*, it seemed, was still living her past glory—and now we were to be part of it.

20.00 The head steward, his chest dignified with two full rows of war ribbons, served us cold drinks in the Observation lounge. The accordion player swung jauntily into Hello Dolly. The *Old Lady* shivered, held her breath. A gentle tremor then took hold and the lights of Southampton began to glide past the tall windows. We were away. A gong sounded and we made prompt tracks for the main restaurant. Caroline and I found ourselves at a circular table laid for seven. The steward eyed us warily as we took our places. The other occupants were a plump young married couple, who were soon to demonstrate insatiable appetites, and three middle-aged ladies. Each of the ladies was travelling alone. One of them, an experienced ocean traveller, who had sailed with the same shipping line to various destinations on three earlier occasions, would soon be putting us wise to the perks and pitfalls. One of the other ladies, a Canary Islands addict, who had twice previously done the identical cruise in the same ship, settled herself placidly to await familiar pleasures.

But the menu was disappointingly limited. Where were the delicacies of yore—the caviare, smoked salmon, oysters, grills and crêpes suzettes? We were at least offered the choice of four or five dishes at each course, described temptingly in French—though, when they reached the table, they looked and tasted as plainly British as could be. And, our table being at the farthest point from the kitchen, the hot ones tended to be served lukewarm and the cold ones tepid. Our steward struggled quietly with his overladen trays. The talk that first evening was primly reticent, for we were still strangers to one another. More hilarious mealtimes lay ahead.

21.45 In the main lounge a team of pursers was conducting bingo. The assembled throng was fast losing its shyness. 'Shake the bag,' rang through the lofty room. 'Bingo,' yelled a rotund red-faced gentleman. Money changed hands, stewards plied their tinkling drinks, and a hubbub of talk and badinage began to rise above the clatter. The orchestra mounted the rostrum and set to work with a quickstep. The officers went swiftly around the room, persuading some of the plainer and older women on to the floor.

The tall purser in his smart evening uniform, jollied us into position for a Paul Jones. In quick succession I danced with a fat bejewelled lady from Lancashire, a grey-haired spinster from London, an enchantingly nimble little girl aged eleven who said she did so wish the party would get a bit more with it, and a young wife who was worried lest her children were not safely asleep in their cabins. There followed a ladies' choice foxtrot for which I was claimed by a formidable middle-aged matron from Birmingham, who was tickled pink to find it all so like a Butlin's holiday but even matier. By now, as waltz followed samba, a good time was being had by all—the ship's officers' stalwart efforts were doing the trick. The *Old Lady* was large enough for those seeking privacy but clearly there was going to be no need for anyone to feel shy or lonely.

DAY TWO   AT SEA

09.00 The ship was rolling lazily. My attentive cabin steward brought breakfast on a tray—fruit, crisp fresh-baked rolls, coffee with cream. Cooked dishes, cereals, juices—all were on call for the asking. Caroline appeared. She was in good form, having survived her first (and only) pangs of seasickness. At about three in the morning, feeling queer, she had rung for the night steward, to be provided with a seasick pill, a cheerful word of encouragement—and that was that. A copy of the ship's newspaper, pushed under the cabin door, brought word from the outside world. The gaily-printed programme for the day offered a tantalising array of fun and enter-tainment. In the morning, for example, deck games, keep-fit hikes, a children's party, a get-together beat session for teenagers, organ music in the lounge, a string trio in the Neptune bar, the accordion in the Observation lounge.

On deck the Bay of Biscay looked grey, and long wind-swept rollers were coming remorselessly at us from the westward. But it was tolerant weather, considering the season and the tradition of that part of the ocean. Towards midday, the sun broke through and pale well-wrapped bodies stretched out on long deck chairs in sheltered areas of the afterdeck spaces. Sea travel makes for hunger, and soup, tea, coffee and biscuits were being dispensed, to still the appetites pending lunch-time guzzles. We came upon Susan, a girl of Caroline's age—I spoke to her, asked her name, the girls liked each other, and they went below decks for a swim. At noon, the siren boomed to tell us the time and the bars began to fill. On the chart the ship's position was marked up. We were nearly four hundred miles from home, half-way across the Bay.

13.30 At lunch, our table companions were noticeably more at ease. The first tentative moans about the food and the service were making themselves quietly heard. As it is a sign of contentment among Britons to find common ground for grumbling, we were obviously well on the road to happiness. The experienced lady told us of the wonderful meals she had consumed in other ships. The regular one said how nice it was to find that the *Old Lady* had not changed her ways but, oh dear, the mutton really was tougher than it used to be. The other lone female said the food, although quite nice, wasn't really up to the standard of the Jersey seafront hotel which she had frequented every summer these past eleven years. The plump young couple wolfed every listed course, expecting each to be an improvement on the last. The ever-smiling head steward came by and asked us pointedly if everything was to our liking. We smiled shyly at him, and said how wonderful it was, and then lowered our eyes, and when he was gone grinned guiltily at one another. The wine steward kept his wily distance, gauging correctly our potential, or lack of it, for his wares.

16.00 Days at sea are busy days. Just time for an afternoon nap, tea to the nostalgic sounds of the palm court orchestra, and into the cinema to see what funny things happened on the way to the forum. Then, a few brisk rounds of the boat deck, a bath and a quick change for dinner, my evening clothes well brushed, the suit hanging ready for use, the bow tie and white shirt laid carefully on the bunk, the black shoes gleaming, all having been made ready by the diligent steward.

22.00 The synthetic horse-racing orgy over, on with the Ladies' Night Dance. 'Ladies!' shrieked the printed programme, 'this is your chance to ask the gentlemen to dance.' Every female was handed a dance programme, with blank spaces in which to write her intended victims' names. A few gentlemen crept stealthily out of the lounge, to take refuge in the bars, but most remained, eyes downcast with becoming modesty. The hostess enjoined all ladies to seize a man and, after dancing, go back with him to his table, light his cigarette, curtsy and withdraw. The music began. Caroline promptly rescued me, as buxom birds of prey fanned out through the crowded room. Then, one of the ship's hostesses claimed me; this made me respectable enough for a blonde and nubile charmer to follow suit, and make me hers for the rest of the session. A bit of luck—she was one of the few attractive young women on board, and now my day-long secret scheming to engineer a chance encounter with her was over. An excellent evening.

DAY THREE   AT SEA

09.30 A gentle sea, bright sunshine and summer temperature. Coatless men and women in sunbathing attire strode the decks or lay roasting gently on their cushioned chairs. What had been a grey featureless mass of humanity at Waterloo a couple of days ago was beginning to assume recognisable shapes and forms. The older men looked younger, the plainer women prettier, the shy children livelier, the grumpy jollier, the pale browner, the rough smoother, the wolves tamer, the timid braver. Shipboard friendships were forming. Parties for drinking, gambling, games-playing, dancing or nattering were assembling. Those seeking love, sex, romance were dating, if not yet mating. For the hearty social climber, for that primly anxious spinster, for the bar stool bore, the card sharper, the salesman—for all those with any kind of aspiration or ambition, the now-or-never period was at hand.

12.00 Noon position directly to the westward of the Straits of Gibraltar, southbound, 23.5 knots, wind NW force 3, sea slight, sky clear, barometer steady.

19.15 The chattering good-humoured queue moved slowly through the doors. An usher called our names, the captain smiled his welcome, pumped our hands, said how nice it was to have us on board. We said how nice it was to be here, the photographer flashed his bulb, the steward brandished a tray of drinks. A purser led us to a group, introduced us and went his affable way. Is this your first voyage, isn't she a gorgeous ship, have you met so-and-so, aren't we lucky with the weather; the clocks go back an hour to-night—an extra hour in bed, an extra hour for drinking; do join us later for the cabaret, poker, dancing, a night cap.

So, from the captain's get-together cocktail party, in our gala-night finery, down the sweeping stairway to the restaurant for the dinner-of-the-week. *Saumon fumé* (at last!) *omelette surprise, dindon farcie atlantique, coupe* Old Lady, *petits fours, vins rouge et blanc en carafe, café americain.* For once, even the experienced lady's complaints were stilled. Jersey and tough mutton were now dead subjects, too. The fat couple grinned, settled their buttocks and went to it with blatant relish. The paper hats came around to be perched above the flushed cheeks and inanely self-conscious grins.

Up by elevator, a quick breather on the promenade deck and into the jam-packed lounge. Garlands between the pillars, streamers, netted balloons awaiting their release, spot lights, fairy lights, a Cole Porter foxtrot, the thronged dance floor. Now, indeed, we were living it up. Cabaret interlude. The assembly was all hushed as a thin balding man followed his heavy-weight white-gowned partner to the microphone. Snatches of operetta and musical comedy excerpts filled the room. The tenor's adam's apple leaped into his collar, the contralto's vast bosoms fought to break out, as the singers reached, crescendo, for the high-note climax of their turn. Ovation. Conjurer—corney patter, bits of tap-dancing, a bawdy song. Ovation.

Then, as the dance orchestra took its well-earned tea break, a lively long-haired loud-playing beat group mounted the stage. We were to be with it at last. Mini-skirted teenagers and young-twenties now jerked and gyrated prettily upon the floor while their elders, firmly seated, nodded benign if uncomprehending approval. Caroline led me firmly into the jungle and kept me busily at it for nearly half-an-hour. The orchestra returned to its duty. The blonde girl joined us, a long cooling drink together, bed-time for Caroline, a couple of languorous dances with the blonde. Midnight. On to the Neptune bar night club. Dimmer lights, cosier atmosphere, sultrier music. Another dance with the blonde. Then, a handsome ship's officer approaches, bows politely, leads her into the crush. Yawn. Settle the bill. A few gulps of sea air. A solitary moment on the empty deck. Full moon, dappling the quiet sea. And so, down the deserted stairway to my cabin—and bed-time for me.

DAY FOUR   LAS PALMAS

11.00 Four tugs nosed the great ship alongside the mole. Hawsers snaked over the water to the bollards, gangways made contact, strings of flags flew up between the masts. Las Palmas. A sunny, summery day. Across the harbour the undistinguished waterfront stretched before us backed by its ugly mass of concrete buildings, but the towering mountains in the distance promised better things to come.

12.30 Early lunch. Cameras, maps and guidebooks at the ready. Talk of pesetas, shopping hours, taxi fares, where to go, what to see. But most of us were booked for set excursions by motor coach. Mine, under the title 'Teror and Arucas', was advertised as a half-day outing. Fare two guineas. 'You will drive through Puerto de la Luz past Canteras Beach,' said the brochure, 'and on through country districts to the typical Canarian village of Teror.' Thence 'to Monte Arucas, from where there are fine views of the coastline. Refreshments will be served . . .'

The coach was airy, clean and high-windowed. Our guide, a lithe brown-skinned girl, began to brief us through her microphone as we set off along the narrow oily jetty, past cargo ships loading timber and bananas, into the town. Soon we were climbing into the foothills. At the first hairpin-bend, a lady at the back announced plaintively that she had no head for heights. We stopped. Conference. Staccato dialogue in Spanish between guide and driver. A passing taxi drew up, the lady entered it, waved, and was gone, back to the port. And just as well. Our coach wound its way higher and higher, swaying into blind corners, its horn blasting round the hair-pin bends, upward to the mountains. Halt. A wander through a banana plantation. But others had preceded us—the litter of ages breeding its filthy flies lay strewn beneath the trees. Onward through the fertile country beside the tomato fields and orange groves and vineyards, under the eucalyptus trees, past clusters of vivid wild geraniums and bougainvillea. Distant glimpses of the sea, vistas of deep valleys, and everywhere the steep forbidding mountains. Glorious, dramatically beautiful country.

Teror. A neat village, its dark pinewood balconies lending a strangely Alpine air. An ornate and tranquil church. Old men taking their siesta in the sun. A few more miles of twisting roads and up, steeply, to the summit of Arucas. Wonderful all-round long distance panoramas. Tea and currant cake in the efficient modern tourist restaurant. The cameras clicked, the souvenir stalls made hay. Then, into the coach and down the tortuous road in convoy with half-a-dozen others, sounding their noisy chorus of horns and klaxons, along the wide valley, past the crowded Canteras Beach to Las Palmas. Pause for eager shopping in a favoured bazaar. Trinkets, cameras, ornaments, and tourist bric-a-brac. Badinage with bystanders, pleasantries with guide and driver. 'You from England? I wish I go there. London big city—my cousin waiter in Fulham. Las Palmas very pretty. You like to see round? I show you Canary village, night club, flamenco, lovely girls.' Back to the jetty. Ten pesetas to the guide. Smiles. Good wishes. Up the rickety gangway, into the familiar reassuring foyer. Dear *Old Lady*. It was so nice to be home.

20.00 Something had happened to the experienced lady. Late to dinner, her cheeks flushed, her eyes bright, she took her seat with a flourish. Oh yes, it certainly had—it had been *quite* a day. In port was a Spanish freighter, a vessel in which she had gone to Tangier a year ago. She happened to be passing, just like that, and imagine her surprise when a familiar voice, a masculine voice, called her name. She looked up and there, on the upper deck, was the chief engineer's robust mustachio'd figure, grinning and waving. So she was bound to go on board, wasn't she, and have the odd glass of vino for old time's sake—well, wouldn't you? What passed during the next two hours, apart from the vino and laughing reminiscences and a bit of cheek pinching, who could tell? We were to be spared the details, thank heavens; the lady's sparkling demeanour was story enough.

And so radiant was she, this usually pallid and self-effacing spinster, that an elderly man at the next table, emboldened, content no longer with brief stolen glances, turned in his seat to smile openly, with devoted fervour.

His reward was a discreet girlish wave, a smile of coy encouragement. Our table was spellbound, as though in the presence of a miracle. We all knew, from casual observation, that the ageing Romeo with the roving eye had with him a fearsome wife who, at the slightest motion of the ship, succumbing to seasickness, took to her bunk. She was for the moment at his side, the ship being in the calm water of the port, but tomorrow evening, in a quiet corner of the boat deck, under the waning moon, as the *Old Lady* lifted gently to the Atlantic swell, might not a trembling passion take its whispering course? Momentarily silent, as she toyed with her *mille feuille* under our watchful gaze, our gallant spinster seemed lost in hopeful thought . . .

22.30 The Spanish folk dancers had performed and gone their way. The band was playing under the fairy lights beneath the stars, on the sports deck. As the sounds of Swinging Britain swept across the dark waters towards Las Palmas city another, more promising romance was blossoming. Among the dancing couples, turning slowly to the music, held tightly in each other's arms were the ship's officer and the young blonde. Except when duty called him these two were now to be inseparable. They seemed well matched, a swarthy bachelor in his early thirties, and the pretty long-legged girl in her late twenties. It was to become her habit, whenever the officer was at his work, to walk or drink or talk with Caroline and me. We were her base and refuge —more aptly, perhaps, her launching pad. But on this night, clearly, she would have no need of our services. At midnight Caroline and I, having had our fill of frolic, made our way below decks to bed.

11.00 A quiet morning. The ship seemed empty, most passengers being ashore. Las Palmas was a short boat ride away across the harbour—a pleasant way to land and one favoured by other cruise ships, but not, alas, by the *Old Lady*. Instead, a long dreary two-mile haul by taxi through the port area and the nondescript traffic-choked suburbs. A stroll through the tawdry streets, some shopping, a look at the replica of a 'typical' Canarian village, a walk by the Canteras Beach, a drink and back on board. Susan, who came with us, and Caroline had become constant companions and, through their friendship, I was now on drinking terms with the parents, a convivial middle-aged couple from the Midlands. For children independent enough to roam on their own and, under the kindly eye of the ship's staff, forage for fun and games, abundantly provided, a cruising liner is the ideal vehicle. Caroline had never had it better.

18.00 The ship's rails were crowded with animated passengers as the *Old Lady* was pulled off the mole to turn slowly in the harbour entrance and head seaward. I was glad to have seen Las Palmas and its striking hinterland, and my curiosity about this popular tourist resort, a mecca for those in search of winter sunshine, was now well satisfied. I cannot say that I fancied the place and to be at large on the ocean once again was no hardship at all.

12.00 Noon position off Morocco, lat 33° 10′ N, long 13° 34′ W, course 017° speed 24 knots, air temp 63°F, sea temp 66°F, baro 30.32 ins falling, wind NE force 3, sea slight, swell NW low, sky part-cloudy, visibility good.

21.30 Carnival night. The long fancy-dress procession wound its noisy way through the crowded festively-decorated lounge. The whole evening had been given up to hilarious preparation. The ship's staff had helped with the loan of bunting, uniforms, musical instruments, costumes discarded on previous voyages, false whiskers, make-up accessories. There were large men dressed as improbably winsome maidens, girls as rollicking sailors, fat women as oriental belly dancers, children as wicked pirates and merry mariners. Caroline and Susan, acting together, represented Port and Starboard, the one dressed all in red and the other in green, wearing sailors' caps, holding before them a cut-out replica of the *Old Lady*'s bows, and weighed down with nautical accoutrements. There was the experienced lady, barely recognisable as Judy, with her ardently tottering paramour, relishing his pink ticket, heavily disguised as Punch. The blonde was there, too, looking ravishingly seductive as a grass-skirted South Seas islander; the eyes of her officer, on duty with the judges, were never off her.

The entrants held the stage in turn, were applauded, withdrew; then the whole lot went hokey-pokeying and conga-ing around the tables to the inspired music of the orchestra, themselves also in fancy dress, while the judges, with due solemnity, weighed their decisions. Then the prizes, the first to a pair ornately attired in the roles of Napoleon and Josephine—and the seventh, happily, to Caroline and Susan. The girls, wide-eyed with pleasure, brought their trophies, two ashtrays bearing a colour picture of the *Old Lady*, to be admired lavishly by their parents.

Then, on with the dance and soon it seemed that the

entire assembly was on the floor entwined with the
streamers, reaching for the balloons, jostling, jiving,
pirouetting, laughing, singing and shouting for joy. No
British reserve here—loud, earthy, uninhibited merry-
making had gripped our whole community. A great party,
a fine evening—a right good time for all.

DAY SEVEN   AT SEA

11.30 The stewards, having done their work in the
quiet aftermath of the revelry, the lounge was sprucely
back to normal. Not a streamer, not a balloon, not a
cigar end, not a blemish to be seen. It was a grey morning
rainy, cold, windswept. The *Old Lady*, creaking amiably
in her joints, was lifting her bows to the rollers, throwing
off the spray, plunging, shivering, rising again in the
breaking seas, down, up, thrusting and twisting her
stately way homeward. In the mid-morning soup queue,
I met the blonde who smiled and said she felt fine, thank
you, and would I please come at noon to meet her
officer? I wandered aft along the promenade deck. At the
far end, well wrapped up, their deck chairs side by side,
the experienced lady and her balding swain, looking
rather the worse for wear, had their heads close together
as they played desultorily with a crossword puzzle.

The blonde and her officer were ensconced in a quiet
corner of the smoking room. They greeted me and
drinks were ordered. I talked to the officer about his
work. When he asked my views about the ship and her
present cruise, I said I was well satisfied apart from the
food and the restaurant service. He explained that, as
cruise passengers, we must expect to be denied the full
treatment. 'The old days are over,' he said. 'Our target
now is the ordinary public, the little men with their

pockets full of cash. We're in it now for profit—no sentiment, no frills, no more VIP treatment. This means lower costs—and lower standards. We can't lose.' I thought they could but was not in the mood for argument. The man in the street is no fool; if it's a Butlin's holiday he wants, he knows where to get the genuine article, at a third the price. And foreigners aren't fools either. The reputation of their ships grows all the time—the French for food, the Germans for service, the Scandinavians for efficiency, the Dutch for ambience, the Italians for gaiety, the Greeks for originality. Britain can only remain best, surely, by continuing to give the best all-round value for money.

The officer went on to say that his was no life for a married man—especially, with a fond smile at the blonde, for a newly married man. The girl said they had it all worked out. He was to complete the ship's present programme of voyages. They would meet when he could get leave between trips, and would consider marriage as soon as he was ready to resign from the company. The officer nodded his assent. 'I am lucky,' he said 'for I can enter the family business whenever I want.' Shipboard romances don't always last; this pair obviously meant to test the durability of theirs. I raised my glass. 'It's an excellent plan,' I said. 'I hope you will invite me to the wedding.' We drank to that and I extricated myself and, leaving them, I went on deck.

20.00 The final evening at sea, and a slight feeling of anti-climax. Was the gloss wearing thin at last? Some passengers were doggedly in evening dress, but most were wearing the clothes in which they would land tomorrow. The Bay of Biscay was being kind to us and there was a full turn-out for dinner. The ship's staff, which had worked

139

so hard for our comfort and enjoyment were relaxing their efforts, as though saving their strength for the *Old Lady*'s next voyage beginning two days hence.

But the usual galaxy of evening entertainment was at our disposal, bingo, horse-racing, cinema, cabaret, dancing and late-night bar service. Gloss or not, the lounge was packed and large parties thronged the bar. At midnight the crowds were still at it, reluctant to go to bed and sleep and awake to find it all behind them. But soon our own party began to disperse—Susan and her parents, the blonde and her officer, Caroline and me. It was nearly one in the morning. A long day lay ahead— and to arrive home weary and bedraggled would be to invite an unwanted if well-deserved rebuke.

DAY EIGHT   SOUTHAMPTON—LONDON

11.30 We have just turned into Southampton Water, after steaming close to the lush green northern shore of the Isle of Wight, with Ryde and Cowes to port, Portsmouth to starboard. It is a bright, crisp, windy morning. The great roadstead of Spithead, once a meeting point of Britain's ironclad armadas, seemed strangely deserted. A solitary destroyer circled languidly, tracking a phantom submarine. A lone yachtsman in yellow wind-cheater, scudding along under reefed mainsail, passed close by our towering ship and waved his greeting.

We pause off the pilot vessel to allow the harbour pilot in his plunging tender to come on board. Now, to port, Fawley refinery, that dense forest of silvery shapes and structures. And ahead, the long waterfront of Southampton docks coming nearer, splashes of colour under the tall cranes emerging gradually into the distinct forms of sleek elegant liners awaiting their departures to faraway continents. The *Old Lady*, with her retinue of tugs and launches, moving at a fair speed, turns smartly towards her berth, hesitates, and runs neatly in, without fuss, to rest gently against the catamarans. Friends and well-wishers wave from the observation platform, bunting streams out in the wind, and great hawsers quiver under the power of the winches, come taut and are made fast.

12.15 A quick walk around, dispensing tips. The traditional rule of thumb is to give a sum equal roughly to five per cent of the fare; for Caroline and me this comes to about £12, the lion's share going to our excellent cabin staff. Down to the restaurant for our last lunch, served briskly by smiling stewards. This is the moment of farewell to the fat young couple, heavy eyed from late-night drinking and a week of guzzling; to the regular lady, looking forward already to her next voyage; to the Jersey addict, now almost converted to ocean travel; and to the experienced one who, having returned her swain to his lawful wife, still glows in the aftermath of her short-lived triumph.

In the lounge, afterwards, fond good-byes to Susan and her parents, Midlands-bound by car. The great tall room is almost empty, chairs and tables stacked to await the cleaners, the stage bare. We seem already to have joined the *Old Lady*'s silent company of ghosts to sail on into the future until, finally, she is rent apart and scattered among the scrapyards, her secrets wafted into oblivion by the mourning winds.

14.00 The young blonde, subdued after taking leave of her officer, joins Caroline and me in the foyer and we go ashore together. The customs officer is tolerant; we descend promptly to the platform and claim our seats in the train. It takes a long time to get to London—more than eight hours, in effect, for our baggage had to be ready outside our staterooms by 09.00 that morning and the boat train is not due at Waterloo until 17.10. Over an hour to wait in the stationary train until at last, huddled in our overcoats, we whistle our way slowly from the docks, craning for a last glimpse of the *Old Lady*'s serene and stately shape, looming high above the quayside. The train lurches over the points and begins the climb inland from the coast. Some heat begins to trickle through the pipes. There is water in the lavatory but the place looks sordid with the grime of yesterday. We have not the heart for a trek to the buffet car. A vaguely familiar figure passes down the corridor; it is the old girl who shared our compartment on the way down but I have not set eyes on her since and wonder what she has been up to all the week. The engine falters and we stop. On again, stop, crawl, stop. We are running late. At last, we rattle our way through the suburbs and enter the straight, heading for Waterloo.

17.40 We draw into the platform. The loud-speaker, in dulcet tones, says how much our late arrival is regretted, this being due to a defective locomotive. Too little and much too late! The shine has worn off, the spell is broken; the *Old Lady* seems already to belong to another distant world. Tempers frayed, there is an impatient rush through the chaos of baggage to the taxi rank. A trickle of cabs. A long queue. We edge our way forward. No cabs, then eight or nine together. Another scramble. Away, at last.

We drive in silence, over the river, and head west. The blonde alights. I see her to her door. We smile and embrace and wish each other luck. But we are almost strangers again, for the alchemy of life afloat is no longer working on us. I rejoin Caroline in the cab. The blonde waves as we draw away, and our last link with the *Old Lady* is severed. It is a melancholy moment, a sad end to our happy week. A short ride through familiar streets; we turn the corner and are home again.

Afterword
Fare Enough

IT has been a sobering experience. If I could now compose my foreword, the tune would be much the same but the tone would be different. It is no longer in me to poke fun at the package tourist. He is the true stoic. No one could be kinder, jollier or better-tempered. Britons abroad may tend to acquiesce over-politely but people who make the best of things, instead of grumbling at every difficulty, make good companions. And they make a good impression on the foreigner.

On the other hand, there are times when a well-aimed brick deserves its place among the bouquets. I think Cherry Burrows (chapter six) was right to blow up in the face of the hotel receptionist; my wife (chapter four) was right to chastise Mr X when her trip was done; and I hope I was right to complain about my coach seat (chapter one), the agents' unhelpfulness (chapters two and five), the double bed (chapter seven) and the food (chapter eight).

All the tours were well managed once they got going. Most remarkable, one was not always made to feel like a mere packaged commodity. But the indifference or inefficiency of some firms at the time of initial enquiry or negotiation was depressing. It is bad business if service at the shop counter does not fulfil the window display's promise. While it is natural to solicit a potential customer's deposit at the first opportunity, it is inexcusable to try to grab it from him before he is sure that he is buying what he really wants.

Since these tours took place, the laws about misrepresentation in sales literature have been tightened up. But there is still a lot of small print on travel application forms which the package tourist may ignore at his peril. What he does not like he should strike out. He should try to ensure, at least, that his deposit will not be forfeit if he has good grounds for a change of plan at reasonable notice, and that he will be compensated if he does not get what he paid for.

If tour promoters deserve blame when they err, they deserve praise equally when they excel. In such a complex and far-reaching trade, at the mercy of politics, weather, mechanical failure and human error, the best laid plans can go astray. That the package tourist gets where he wants to be on time, and fares as well as he does as often as he does, and comes home safely, and is usually well satisfied, is fair tribute to the skill and competence of all who serve him.

Tourism is a fast-growing business and there seems to be no end to it. Each year, the enterprise and enthusiasm of tour promoters offer new bargains, new excitements, new destinations. But the bulk of their turnover is the great mass of old well-tried favourites, sometimes with new frills, improved facilities and more jaunting for the money. As volume rises, some prices are actually falling; in particular, many longer-distance all-inclusive tours by air now cost substantially less than the scheduled air fare alone. By the time this book is printed, one or other of the tours it describes may well be available more cheaply.

I should make clear, perhaps, that less expensive variations of nearly all these tours were obtainable anyway for the asking. Those reported in chapters two, four and five could have been booked through the same operators at much lower cost if charter or night flights and simpler accommodation had been chosen; humbler cabins were available on the cruise in chapter eight; and tours rather like those described in chapters one, six and seven, but with harder going, were on offer at lower prices by other operators. While the independent traveller could have gone it alone, for much the same outlay, on at least three trips given in this book, he could not hope financially to better any of the cheaper versions.

Alas, the spread of tourism is queering his pitch in more ways than that. Pressure of demand, extension of facilities and the pared-down costs of bulk travel are taking the hordes farther and farther afield, while the blight of standardised resorts and mass-produced amenities and queueing cars and shuffling sightseers spreads remorselessly across familiar lands. Spice and variety and adventure are fast going out of travel. One place will soon be like every other, until it will no longer be cause for surprise, as in chapter four, that Italian food and the Italian language are hard to come by in an Italian hotel.

Will the dull uniformity of large-scale package tourism eventually prove self-defeating? I doubt it. Change of venue, of climate and of workaday habit is always refreshing; the idea of 'going abroad' will always appeal and, hopefully, impress the neighbours. Above all, there is the prospect of new friendships, or of romance.

I have to admit that my own life was not changed by the coach trip in chapter one or by any of my other tours and, by all accounts, those who went about my business on the remainder suffered the same immunity. The single lady who shared my seat in that coach was very charming and I enjoyed her company but I am sure it did not occur to either of us that we might be meant for one another. No doubt, of the holidays covered by this book, the ski party and the ocean cruise are the most promising media for the lonely and the lovelorn, liaisons like those recorded in chapter eight being normal currency afloat. But the *Old Lady* herself can oblige no longer; sadly, unable to pay her way, she is to be taken out of service. The line to Southampton having since been electrified, I hope that grisly boat train has been taken out of service, too.

My stint is done, and I fear it has not converted me. I am not package tour material. I wish it could be otherwise but, for me, in the holiday season, there is no place like home.

Appendix
List of Tour Promoters

In the end, I examined the literature of more than fifty London-based tour operators and travel agents. Of these firms, half were later approached by telephone or personal visit. Finally, the tours described in this book were booked through the following—to all of whom gratitude is due, at least, for a good deal of fun and for our safe homecomings:

Apal Travel, 78 New Oxford Street, W1.
Ashton & Mitchell Travel, 2 Old Bond Street, W1
Clarkson's Tours, 17 Sun Street, EC2.
Continental Villas, 38 Sloane Street, SW1.
Thos. Cook & Son, Berkeley Street, W1.

Murison Small, 3 St George Street, W1.
Ramblers' Association, 124 Finchley Road, NW3.
National Union of Students, 3 Endsleigh Street, WC1.

Among those with whom I was unable, this time, to do business, the undermentioned deserve praise for the notably courteous and efficient way in which they dealt with my enquiries:

Bachelors Abroad, 85 Duke Street, W1.
Glenton Tours, 397 Queens Road, SE14.
Global Tours, 301 Oxford Street, W1.
F & W Ingham, 26 Old Bond Street, W1.
Lord Brothers, 54 Regent Street, W1.
Maltavillas, 10 Holland Road, W14.
Montague Shaw, 44 Marylebone High Street, W1.
Rentavilla, 40 Piccadilly, W1.
Whatley Whittaker, 10 Duke Street, W1.

BRITISH
ISLES

DENMA

London

HOLLAND

Utrecht

G E R

Brussels

BELGIUM

Bad
Ems

Paris

Feldberg

FRANCE

Lucerne

Autun

Interlaken

SWITZ

Zermatt

PORTUGAL

Sitges

S P A I N

Palma

*Las
Palmas*

MAIN DESTINATIONS
AND OVERNIGHT STOPS

For Product Safety Concerns and Information please contact our EU
representative GPSR@taylorandfrancis.com
Taylor & Francis Verlag GmbH, Kaufingerstraße 24, 80331 München, Germany

www.ingramcontent.com/pod-product-compliance
Lightning Source LLC
Chambersburg PA
CBHW070244290326
41929CB00046B/2448